# The Latest Air Fryer Cookbook for UK 2024

1800+ Days Affordable and Healthy Air Fryer Recipes to Satisfy Your Family's Favorites with Air Fryer Guide For Beginners

*Gertha D. Ewald*

# Copyright© 2024 By Gertha D. Ewald
# All Rights Reserved

This book is copyright protected. It is only for personal use. You cannot amend, distribute, sell, use, quote or paraphrase any part of the content within this book, without the consent of the author or publisher. Under no circumstances will any blame or legal responsibility be held against the publisher, or author, for any damages, reparation, or monetary loss due to the information contained within this book, either directly or indirectly.

**Disclaimer Notice:**

Please note the information contained within this document is for educational and entertainment purposes only. All effort has been executed to present accurate, up to date, reliable, complete information. No warranties of any kind are declared or implied. Readers acknowledge that the author is not engaged in the rendering of legal, financial, medical or professional advice. The content within this book has been derived from various sources. Please consult a licensed professional before attempting any techniques outlined in this book. By reading this document, the reader agrees that under no circumstances is the author responsible for any losses, direct or indirect, that are incurred as a result of the use of the information contained within this document, including, but not limited to, errors, omissions, or inaccuracies.

# Contents

Introduction ............................................................................................... 1

## Chapter 1: Breakfast ............................................................. 5

Crispy Cinnamon French Toast Sticks ................................................. 5
Golden Hash Brown Bites ..................................................................... 5
Air Fryer Bacon and Egg Cups ............................................................. 5
Fluffy Blueberry Pancake Muffins ........................................................ 5
Sausage and Cheese Stuffed Croissant ................................................. 6
Cheesy Mushroom and Spinach Omelette ............................................ 6
Apple Cinnamon Breakfast Pastries ..................................................... 6
English Breakfast Potato Rosti ............................................................. 7
Maple Glazed Breakfast Sausages ........................................................ 7
Crispy Baked Avocado Toast ................................................................ 7
Banana-Stuffed French Toast Pockets .................................................. 7
Savory Spinach and Feta Breakfast Wraps .......................................... 8
Air Fryer Breakfast Pizza ..................................................................... 8
Cinnamon Sugar Donut Holes .............................................................. 8
Mediterranean Style Shakshuka ........................................................... 9
Parmesan Crusted Breakfast Potatoes .................................................. 9
Raspberry Cream Cheese Stuffed French Toast .................................. 9
Cheese and Ham Breakfast Quesadilla ............................................... 10
Air Fryer Churro Waffles ................................................................... 10
English Muffin Breakfast Sandwiches ............................................... 10
Air Fryer Breakfast Tostadas Recipe ................................................. 11
Air Fryer Cinnamon Sugar Churros .................................................. 11
Banana & Peanut butter Bagel ........................................................... 12
Air Fryer Breakfast Sweet Rolls ........................................................ 12
Air Fryer Breakfast Tostadas Recipe ................................................. 12
Traditional English Breakfast ............................................................. 13
Omelette .............................................................................................. 13
French Toast ....................................................................................... 13

## Chapter 2: Lunch ............................................................... 14

Crispy Fish and Chips ......................................................................... 14
Spicy Chicken Tikka Skewers ............................................................ 14
Mediterranean Stuffed Bell Peppers ................................................... 14

Air Fried Veggie Quesadillas ...............................................................................................15
Pesto Chicken Panini Melts ..................................................................................................15
Crunchy Falafel Balls ...........................................................................................................15
Air Fryer Beef and Vegetable Kebabs...................................................................................16
Sticky Teriyaki Tofu .............................................................................................................16
Cheese and Bacon Stuffed Mushrooms ................................................................................16
Sweet Potato and Chickpea Patties .......................................................................................17
Air Fryer Chicken Caesar Wraps ..........................................................................................17
Pork and Apple Sausage Rolls ..............................................................................................17
Tex-Mex Loaded Nachos ......................................................................................................18
Air Fryer Caprese Stuffed Chicken Breast ...........................................................................18
Crispy Coconut Shrimp ........................................................................................................18
Air Fried Falafel Wraps ........................................................................................................19
Spinach and Feta Stuffed Portobello Mushrooms ................................................................19
Sticky Hoisin Glazed Salmon ...............................................................................................19
Air Fryer BBQ Pork Ribs .....................................................................................................20
Cheesy Broccoli Bites...........................................................................................................20
Chicken Biryani ....................................................................................................................20
Air Fryer Buffalo Chicken Wings ........................................................................................21
Air Fryer Chicken Tikka Skewers ........................................................................................21
Air Fryer Duck Breast with Orange Glaze ...........................................................................21
Honey Garlic Pork Chops .....................................................................................................22
Air Fryer BBQ Ribs ..............................................................................................................22
Air Fryer Bacon Wrapped Avocados ....................................................................................22
Kung Pao Chicken .................................................................................................................23
Honey Mustard Air Fryer Chicken Drumsticks ...................................................................23

## Chapter 3: Dinner ...............................................................................................................24

Balsamic Glazed Air Fryer Pork Tenderloin ........................................................................24
Air Fried Lemon Herb Chicken Thighs ................................................................................24
Crispy Coconut-Crusted Cod Fillets .....................................................................................24
Stuffed Peppers with Quinoa and Black Beans ....................................................................24
Honey Mustard Glazed Air Fryer Lamb Chops ...................................................................25
Air Fried Veggie and Chickpea Curry..................................................................................25
Air Fryer Beef Stir-Fry with Mixed Vegetables ..................................................................25
Buttermilk Fried Air Fryer Chicken .....................................................................................26
Sticky Maple Glazed Air Fryer Salmon ...............................................................................26
Air Fried Veggie Frittata .......................................................................................................26
Air Fryer Turkey Meatballs with Marinara Sauce ...............................................................27

Mediterranean Style Air Fryer Lamb Kebabs ........................................................................... 27
Stuffed Portobello Mushrooms with Spinach and Goat Cheese ............................................. 27
Air Fried Honey Garlic Tofu ..................................................................................................... 27
Pesto and Mozzarella Stuffed Air Fryer Chicken Breasts ....................................................... 28
BBQ Pulled Pork Sliders ........................................................................................................... 28
Crispy Garlic Parmesan Air Fryer Brussels Sprouts ............................................................... 28
Jamaican Jerk Chicken Wings .................................................................................................. 29
Air Fryer Beef and Broccoli ...................................................................................................... 29
Cheesy Cauliflower Bake .......................................................................................................... 29
Air Fryer Sticky Orange Ginger Glazed Duck Breast ............................................................. 29
Stuffed Zucchini Boats with Ground Turkey and Cheese ....................................................... 30
Crispy Coconut-Curry Air Fryer Prawns ................................................................................. 30
Air Fried Balsamic Glazed Veggie Skewers ............................................................................. 30
Garlic Parmesan Crusted Air Fryer Lamb Chops ................................................................... 31
Tex-Mex Air Fryer Stuffed Peppers .......................................................................................... 31
Lemon-Herb Butter Air Fryer Lobster Tails ............................................................................ 31
Air Fried Chicken Cordon Bleu ................................................................................................ 32
Crispy Breaded Air Fryer Pork Schnitzel ................................................................................ 32
Vegan Air Fryer Tofu Tikka Masala ......................................................................................... 32
Air Fryer Teriyaki Glazed Beef Skewers .................................................................................. 33
Moroccan Spiced Air Fryer Chickpea Stew ............................................................................. 33
Air Fried Stuffed Portobello Mushroom Caps with Sun-Dried Tomatoes ............................. 33
BBQ Pulled Jackfruit Sandwiches ............................................................................................ 34
Air Fryer Honey Mustard Glazed Turkey Breast .................................................................... 34
Herbed Air Fried Rack of Lamb ............................................................................................... 34
Crispy Air Fryer Polenta Fries .................................................................................................. 35
Jamaican Jerk Air Fryer Pork Tenderloin ............................................................................... 35
Mediterranean Style Air Fryer Veggie Platter with Tzatziki .................................................. 35
Sticky Maple Glazed Air Fryer Duck Legs ............................................................................... 36
Air Fryer Lemon Pepper Chicken Breasts ............................................................................... 36
Air Fryer Whole Roasted Chicken ............................................................................................ 36
Chicken and Wild Mushroom Pie ............................................................................................. 37
BBQ Glazed Air Fryer Ribs ....................................................................................................... 37
Italian Seasoned Air Fryer Meatballs ...................................................................................... 38
Lamb Tagine .............................................................................................................................. 38

## Chapter 4: Beef, Pork, And Lamb ............................................................................ 39

Air Fryer Rosemary Garlic Lamb Chops ................................................................................. 39
Beef and Guinness Pie Pockets ................................................................................................. 39

Pork Belly Burnt Ends ................................................................................................. 39
Air Fried Lamb Kofta Kebabs with Mint Yoghurt Dip ............................................. 40
Spiced Beef Samosas .................................................................................................. 40
Honey Glazed Air Fryer Pork Loin............................................................................. 40
Air Fryer Beef Wellington Bites ................................................................................. 41
Garlic-Herb Crusted Air Fryer Rack of Lamb .......................................................... 41
Pork and Apple Stuffing Balls.................................................................................... 41
Shepherd's Pie Stuffed Peppers ................................................................................. 42
Lamb and Apricot Skewers with Tzatziki ................................................................. 42
Sticky Maple Glazed Air Fryer Pork Ribs ................................................................. 43
Air Fried Beef and Mushroom Pies ........................................................................... 43
Asian Style Air Fryer Beef Stir-Fry ........................................................................... 43
 BBQ Rubbed Air Fryer Pork Ribs ............................................................................. 44
 Smoked Pork Ribs ...................................................................................................... 44
Chuck Kebab with Rocket ......................................................................................... 45
Italian Lamb Chops with Avocado Mayo ................................................................. 45
Spicy Rump Steak ....................................................................................................... 45

## Chapter 5: Fish And Seafood ................................................................. 46

Air Fryer Lemon-Herb Crusted Cod Fillets ............................................................. 46
Panko-Crusted Air Fried Scallops ............................................................................ 46
Smoked Paprika Air Fryer Prawns ........................................................................... 46
Air Fried Garlic Butter Lobster Tails ........................................................................ 46
Crispy Coconut-Crusted Air Fryer Haddock ........................................................... 47
Sea Bass with Mediterranean Herbs ......................................................................... 47
Lemon-Dill Air Fryer Salmon Patties........................................................................ 47
Tempura-style Air Fried King Prawns ...................................................................... 48
Air Fryer Cajun Tilapia .............................................................................................. 48
Garlic and Parmesan Crusted Air Fryer Mussels .................................................... 48
Tandoori Marinated Air Fryer Monkfish.................................................................. 49
Crispy Salt and Pepper Squid .................................................................................... 49
Grilled Garlic and Herb King Prawns....................................................................... 49
Creamy Garlic Butter Mussels .................................................................................. 50
Southern-Style Catfish ............................................................................................... 50
Coconut Cream Mackerel .......................................................................................... 50
Mediterranean Grilled Whole Fish ........................................................................... 51
Lemon Garlic Shrimp Skewers .................................................................................. 51
Bang Bang Shrimp ...................................................................................................... 51
Grilled Garlic Butter Lobster Tails ........................................................................... 52

## Chapter 6: Sides & Appetisers ..................................................................... 53

Air Fryer Garlic Parmesan Courgette Chips .................................................................. 53
Crispy Air Fried Halloumi Fries .................................................................................... 53
Pesto-Stuffed Air Fryer Mushrooms ............................................................................. 53
Air Fried Sweet Potato Wedges with Rosemary ........................................................... 54
Tempura-style Air Fryer Green Beans ......................................................................... 54
Stuffed Jalapeño Peppers with Cream Cheese ............................................................ 54
Air Fryer Balsamic Glazed Brussels Sprouts ............................................................... 54
Crispy Air Fried Polenta Bites with Marinara Dip ......................................................... 55
Paprika and Lime Air Fryer Corn on the Cob ............................................................... 55
Air Fried Butternut Squash Fritters ............................................................................... 55
TORTILLA CHIPS .......................................................................................................... 55
RANCH MOZZARELLA STICKS .................................................................................. 56
Bruschetta with Tomato and Basil ................................................................................ 56
Authentic Scotch Eggs ................................................................................................. 56
Rumaki ......................................................................................................................... 57
 Porridge Bread ............................................................................................................ 57

## Chapter 7: Vegan And Veggie ........................................................................ 58

Air Fried Vegan Falafel Patties .................................................................................... 58
Crispy Stuffed Portobello Mushrooms with Spinach and Vegan Cheese ..................... 58
Air Fryer Veggie Spring Rolls ....................................................................................... 58
Vegan Buffalo Cauliflower Bites ................................................................................... 59
Air Fried Stuffed Peppers with Quinoa and Black Beans ............................................. 59
Chickpea and Spinach Vegan Tikka Masala ................................................................ 59
Air Fryer Vegan Sweet Potato and Chickpea Curry ..................................................... 60
Crispy Coconut-Crusted Tofu Nuggets ......................................................................... 60
Vegan Air Fried Courgette Fritters ............................................................................... 60
Air Fryer Vegan Stuffed Grape Leaves ........................................................................ 61
Vegan Air Fried Falafel Wraps with Tahini Sauce ........................................................ 61
Air Fried Vegan Onion Bhajis ....................................................................................... 61
Crispy Air Fryer Tofu Satay Skewers ........................................................................... 62
Air Fried Vegan Breakfast Burritos ............................................................................... 62
Spicy Cauliflower Wings ............................................................................................... 62
Air-Fried Mediterranean Vegetables ............................................................................. 63
Brussels Sprouts with Balsamic Glaze ......................................................................... 63
Curried Fruit .................................................................................................................. 64
 Roasted Aubergine ...................................................................................................... 64
Air Fryer Sweet Potato and Black Bean Cakes ............................................................ 64

## Chapter 8: Sweet Snacks And Desserts ... 65

Air Fryer Apple Cinnamon Fritters ... 65
Chocolate-stuffed Air Fried Croissants ... 65
Air Fried Banoffee Pie Bites ... 65
Sticky Toffee Pudding Cups ... 65
Air Fryer Lemon Blueberry Scones ... 66
Vegan Air Fried Donuts with Raspberry Glaze ... 66
Air Fryer Baklava Rolls ... 67
Mini Victoria Sponge Cakes ... 67
Air Fryer Pear and Almond Tarts ... 67
Caramelized Banana Spring Rolls ... 67
Air Fried Sticky Rice Mango Pudding ... 68
Blueberry-Lemon Bread Pudding ... 68
Air Fryer Raspberry White Chocolate Cookies ... 68
Air Fried Chocolate Covered Strawberries ... 69
Apple Crumble Stuffed Baked Apples ... 69
Air Fried Churro Bites with Cinnamon Sugar ... 69
Air Fryer Pecan Pie Pockets ... 69
Vegan Air Fried Coconut Macaroons ... 70
Air Fryer Orange Glazed Madeleines ... 70
Peach and Raspberry Galette ... 70
Baked Apples and Walnuts ... 71
Brown Sugar Banana Bread ... 71

## References ... 72

# Introduction

Welcome to the world of air frying – a revolutionary cooking method that's changing the way we prepare delicious meals! In this cookbook, designed especially for beginners, you're about to embark on a culinary journey that combines convenience, health, and incredible flavours.

Air frying has taken the UK by storm, offering a healthier alternative to traditional frying while still producing mouthwatering, crispy results. Whether you're a novice in the kitchen or an experienced home cook looking to explore new techniques, this cookbook is your go-to resource for mastering the art of air frying.

Inside these pages, you'll find an array of simple yet tantalizing recipes tailored for the trusty air fryer. From appetizers to mains, sides, and even delightful desserts, each recipe is carefully crafted to help you navigate your way through this innovative cooking appliance with ease.

Discover how the air fryer can transform everyday ingredients into crispy, golden delights using significantly less oil than conventional frying methods. Unleash its potential to cook a variety of dishes faster, all while maintaining the natural flavours and textures of your favourite foods.

Throughout this cookbook, you'll learn valuable tips, cooking times, and techniques that will build your confidence and inspire your creativity in the kitchen. Get ready to embark on a culinary adventure that promises healthier, tastier meals with every bite.

Join us on this exciting journey into the world of air frying, where convenience meets culinary excellence, making cooking at home simpler, healthier, and undoubtedly more enjoyable!

## What is an Air Fryer?

An air fryer is a kitchen appliance that revolutionizes cooking by employing rapid air technology to prepare food. Unlike traditional deep frying methods that submerge food in oil, an air fryer uses hot air circulation to cook meals, creating a crispy outer layer while maintaining moisture inside. This innovative device is designed with a heating mechanism and a high-powered fan, which circulates hot air at high speeds around the food, creating a crispy texture similar to frying but with significantly less oil or even none at all.

Air fryers are versatile and can be used to cook a wide range of dishes, from crispy fries and crunchy snacks to succulent meats, flavorful vegetables, and even desserts. They offer a healthier alternative to deep frying, reducing the amount of oil used in cooking while still achieving that desirable crispy finish. Additionally, air fryers are known for their convenience, often requiring shorter cooking times compared to traditional cooking methods, making them an ideal kitchen companion for busy individuals and families.

The appeal of an air fryer lies not only in its ability to create healthier versions of favourite fried foods but also in its ease of use and versatility. With precise temperature controls and cooking settings, it's an appliance that allows users to explore various recipes and experiment with different cooking techniques, providing an enjoyable and efficient cooking experience for both beginners and seasoned cooks alike.

## Why Use an Air Fryer?

Using an air fryer offers numerous advantages that make it a worthwhile addition to any kitchen. Here are some compelling reasons why people choose to use an air fryer:

- Healthier Cooking: One of the primary reasons to use an air fryer is its ability to cook food

with significantly less oil than traditional frying methods. It promotes healthier eating habits by reducing overall fat intake, making it an appealing option for those looking to cut down on excess oil in their diet.
- Versatility: Air fryers are incredibly versatile appliances that can cook a wide range of foods. From crispy fries and golden chicken wings to roasted vegetables and even baked goods, the air fryer's versatility allows for various cooking methods, making it suitable for preparing diverse recipes.
- Time Efficiency: Air fryers are known for their quick cooking times. They heat up rapidly and cook food faster than conventional ovens, reducing overall cooking times for many dishes. This time-saving feature is particularly beneficial for busy individuals or families seeking efficient meal preparation.
- Easy to Use and Clean: Air fryers are user-friendly appliances, often equipped with intuitive controls and pre-programmed settings for different recipes. Additionally, they require minimal cleanup compared to traditional frying methods, as they produce less grease and typically have removable, dishwasher-safe parts.
- Energy Efficient: These appliances generally consume less energy than conventional ovens or stovetops, contributing to lower electricity usage and potentially reducing energy bills over time.
- Reduced Odour: Unlike traditional frying methods that can leave lingering cooking odours in the kitchen, air fryers tend to minimize cooking smells, making them an attractive option for households looking to maintain a fresher environment.

Overall, the convenience, health benefits, and versatility of air fryers make them a popular choice for home cooks seeking an efficient, healthier, and more convenient way to prepare a variety of delicious meals.

## How to Choose an Air Fryer

When selecting an air fryer, consider several factors to find the right one that suits your needs and preferences:
- Capacity: Determine the ideal size based on your typical meal portions. Air fryers come in various sizes, typically measured by quart capacity. For individuals or small families, a 3-4 quart capacity might suffice, while larger families might prefer a 5-6 quart or larger size.
- Cooking Functions and Presets: Look for models offering versatile cooking functions and preset programs. Some air fryers have preset options for specific foods, making it simpler to cook various dishes with just the touch of a button.
- Temperature and Timer Control: Ensure the air fryer offers precise temperature control and a timer for accurate cooking. Models with adjustable temperature settings ranging from 180°C to 200°C and timers up to 60 minutes provide flexibility for different recipes.
- Ease of Cleaning: Opt for air fryers with dishwasher-safe components, detachable baskets, and non-stick coatings. Removable parts make cleaning more convenient and efficient.
- Additional Features: Consider additional features that might enhance your cooking experience, such as digital displays, preheating functions, and accessories like baking pans, racks, or skewers that can expand cooking possibilities.
- Brand and Reviews: Research reputable brands known for quality and durability. Read customer reviews to gain insights into real-life experiences and determine which models align with your requirements.
- Budget: Set a budget and find an air fryer that offers a balance between price and features. There's a range of options available, from budget-friendly models to more advanced, feature-rich appliances.

By considering these factors, you can choose an air fryer that best suits your cooking preferences, kitchen space, and lifestyle, ensuring an enjoyable and efficient cooking experience.

## Air Fryer Tips and Tricks

Mastering the art of air frying involves learning a few tips and tricks that can elevate your culinary experience:
- Preheat the Air Fryer: Just like an oven, preheating the air fryer for a few minutes before cooking helps achieve better results. It ensures

even cooking and quicker crisping.
- Use Oil Wisely: While air frying reduces the need for excessive Oil, lightly spraying or brushing a small amount of Oil on food items can enhance crispiness and browning.
- Don't Overcrowd the Basket: Ensure proper airflow by arranging food items in a single layer without overcrowding the basket. This allows hot air to circulate evenly, resulting in evenly cooked dishes.
- Shake or Flip Foods: For even cooking and browning, periodically shake or flip the food halfway through the cooking process. It helps achieve uniform crispness on all sides.
- Experiment with Temperature and Timing: Not all foods require the same temperature or cooking time. Experiment with temperature settings and cooking times to find the perfect balance for different dishes.
- Use Parchment Paper or Foil: When cooking foods that might drip or create a mess, consider using parchment paper or aluminium foil at the bottom of the basket. This makes cleaning up easier.
- Use Accessories Smartly: Some air fryers come with additional accessories like racks, skewers, or baking pans. Experiment with these accessories to diversify the types of dishes you can prepare.
- Monitor Food: Keep an eye on your food, especially during the first few uses. This helps you become familiar with how your air fryer cooks different foods and prevents overcooking.
- Adjust Recipes for Air Frying: While many oven recipes can be adapted for an air fryer, some adjustments might be needed. Consider reducing temperatures or cooking times slightly when converting recipes.
- Clean Regularly: After each use, clean your air fryer thoroughly, following the manufacturer's instructions. Regular maintenance ensures longevity and prevents lingering odours or flavours.

Adopting these tips and tricks will not only improve your air frying skills but also broaden the range of delicious, healthier meals you can effortlessly prepare in your air fryer.

## How to Clean and Maintain Your Air Fryer

Keeping your air fryer clean and well-maintained is crucial for its longevity and the quality of your cooking. Here are steps to ensure your air fryer stays in top condition:

- Unplug and Cool Down: Always ensure the air fryer is unplugged and completely cooled down before cleaning.
- Removable Parts: Most air fryers have detachable components like baskets, trays, and racks. Remove these parts carefully to wash them separately.
- Hand Wash or Dishwasher: Check the manufacturer's instructions to determine if the parts are dishwasher-safe. If not, hand wash them with warm, soapy water. Use a non-abrasive sponge or cloth to avoid damaging the non-stick coating.
- Remove Food Residues: For stubborn residues, soak the parts in warm, soapy water for a few minutes before cleaning. Avoid using abrasive cleaners or tools that can scratch the surface.
- Clean the Interior: Use a damp cloth to wipe down the interior walls and heating element of the air fryer. Be gentle and cautious around the heating element.
- Dry Thoroughly: After washing, ensure all parts are completely dry before reassembling or storing to prevent moisture buildup, which can lead to mould or mildew.
- Clean the Exterior: Wipe the exterior of the air fryer with a damp cloth. Avoid using harsh chemicals or abrasive cleaners, as they may damage the surface.
- Regular Maintenance: Regularly check for accumulated grease or food debris in the basket or trays. Promptly clean these areas to prevent odours and ensure optimal performance.
- Store Properly: Store your air fryer in a clean, dry place, away from direct sunlight and moisture. Make sure it's completely dry before storage.
- Follow Manufacturer's Guidelines: Always refer to the manufacturer's manual for specific cleaning instructions and maintenance tips tailored to your air fryer model.

By following these cleaning and maintenance practices, you'll not only keep your air fryer in good condition but also ensure that it continues to produce delicious and healthy meals for years to come.

## Air Fryer FAQs

Here are some common FAQs about air fryers:

What exactly is an air fryer?

An air fryer is a kitchen appliance that cooks by circulating hot air around the food at high speed, giving it a crispy texture similar to deep-frying but using significantly less oil or even none at all.

How does an air fryer work?

Air fryers use a heating element and a fan to circulate hot air around the food inside a cooking chamber. This rapid air movement cooks the food and creates a crispy outer layer.

What can you cook in an air fryer?

Air fryers are versatile and can cook a wide range of foods, including but not limited to, vegetables, meats, poultry, seafood, frozen foods, and even baked goods like cakes or muffins.

Is it healthier to cook with an air fryer?

Air fryers typically use less oil than traditional frying methods, reducing the overall fat content in foods. This can make certain dishes healthier, but the nutritional value also depends on the ingredients used and the cooking method.

Can I use aluminium foil or parchment paper in an air fryer?

Yes, you can use aluminium foil or parchment paper in your air fryer basket, but it's important to follow the manufacturer's guidelines and ensure that they don't obstruct the airflow. This helps to prevent interference with the cooking process.

Can I open the air fryer while it's cooking?

Yes, most air fryers allow you to open the cooking chamber during the cooking process to check on the food or to add seasoning. However, doing this might affect the cooking time and temperature, so try to minimize the frequency of opening the fryer.

How do I prevent food from sticking in the air fryer basket?

To prevent sticking, lightly coat the basket or trays with oil or cooking spray before placing the food in them. Avoid overcrowding the basket, as this can cause uneven cooking and sticking.

Are air fryers easy to clean?

Air fryers are generally easy to clean, especially those with removable and dishwasher-safe parts. Regular cleaning after each use and following the manufacturer's cleaning instructions will help maintain the air fryer's cleanliness.

These FAQs cover some common queries about air fryers. Remember, it's always best to refer to your specific air fryer's manual for detailed instructions and guidelines tailored to your appliance.

# Chapter 1: Breakfast

## Crispy Cinnamon French Toast Sticks

Serves: 4
Prep time: 10 minutes / Cook time: 8 minutes

**Ingredients:**
- 8 slices of white bread, cut into sticks
- 2 large eggs
- 60ml whole milk
- 2 tbsp granulated sugar
- 1 tsp ground cinnamon
- 1/2 tsp vanilla extract
- Cooking spray or oil, for greasing

**Preparation instructions:**
1. Preheat the Air Fryer to 180°C for 5 minutes.
2. In a shallow bowl, whisk together eggs, milk, sugar, cinnamon, and vanilla extract.
3. Dip each bread stick into the egg mixture, ensuring they're coated evenly.
4. Lightly grease the air fryer basket with cooking spray or oil.
5. Place the coated bread sticks in the basket, making sure they are not touching.
6. Air fry at 180°C for about 8 minutes or until golden brown and crispy.
7. Serve warm with maple syrup or your preferred toppings.

## Golden Hash Brown Bites

Serves: 4
Prep time: 10 minutes / Cook time: 12 minutes

**Ingredients:**
- 400g shredded potatoes
- 2 tbsp olive oil
- 1/2 tsp garlic powder
- 1/2 tsp onion powder
- Salt and black pepper, to taste
- Cooking spray or oil, for greasing

**Preparation instructions:**
1. Preheat the Air Fryer to 190°C for 5 minutes.
2. In a bowl, mix shredded potatoes with olive oil, garlic powder, onion powder, salt, and pepper.
3. Grease the air fryer basket lightly with cooking spray or oil.
4. Scoop potato mixture and form small bite-sized balls.
5. Place the hash brown bites into the air fryer basket, ensuring they're not overcrowded.
6. Air fry at 190°C for about 12 minutes or until crispy and golden brown.
7. Remove from the air fryer and serve hot.

## Air Fryer Bacon and Egg Cups

Serves: 4
Prep time: 10 minutes / Cook time: 12 minutes

**Ingredients:**
- 8 slices bacon
- 4 large eggs
- Salt and black pepper, to taste
- Chopped fresh herbs (optional)

**Preparation instructions:**
1. Preheat the Air Fryer to 180°C for 5 minutes.
2. Line each cup of the air fryer baking pan with a slice of bacon, creating a cup shape.
3. Crack an egg into each bacon cup.
4. Season with salt and pepper, and sprinkle with chopped fresh herbs if desired.
5. Place the baking pan in the air fryer basket.
6. Air fry at 180°C for about 12 minutes or until the eggs are set to your desired doneness.
7. Remove from the air fryer, let cool slightly, and serve.

## Fluffy Blueberry Pancake Muffins

Makes: 8 muffins
Prep time: 15 minutes / Cook time: 10 minutes

**Ingredients:**
- 150g plain flour
- 1 tbsp baking powder
- 2 tbsp granulated sugar
- 1 egg
- 180ml whole milk
- 2 tbsp melted butter

- 100g blueberries

**Preparation instructions:**
1. Preheat the Air Fryer to 180°C for 5 minutes.
2. In a bowl, whisk together flour, baking powder, and sugar.
3. In another bowl, beat the egg, then add milk and melted butter, stirring until combined.
4. **Gradually add the wet Ingredients: to the dry Ingredients:, mixing until just combined.**
5. Gently fold in the blueberries.
6. Grease muffin cups or use silicone liners and fill each cup 3/4 full with the batter.
7. Place the muffin cups in the air fryer basket.
8. Air fry at 180°C for about 10 minutes or until the muffins are golden and a toothpick inserted comes out clean.
9. Allow them to cool for a few minutes before serving.

## Sausage and Cheese Stuffed Croissant

Serves: 4
Prep time: 10 minutes / Cook time: 10 minutes

**Ingredients:**
- 1 sheet ready-to-roll croissant dough
- 8 cooked breakfast sausages, halved lengthwise
- 60g shredded cheddar cheese
- 1 egg, beaten (for egg wash)

**Preparation instructions:**
1. Preheat the Air Fryer to 180°C for 5 minutes.
2. Unroll the croissant dough and separate it into triangles.
3. Place half a sausage and a sprinkle of shredded cheddar cheese at the wider end of each triangle.
4. Roll the dough around the sausage and cheese, tucking in the edges.
5. Brush each croissant with beaten egg for a golden finish.
6. Place the stuffed croissants in the air fryer basket, ensuring they're not touching.
7. Air fry at 180°C for about 10 minutes or until golden brown and cooked through.
8. Remove from the air fryer and let cool slightly before serving.

## Cheesy Mushroom and Spinach Omelette

Serves: 2
Prep time: 10 minutes / Cook time: 8 minutes

**Ingredients:**
- 4 large eggs
- 60ml whole milk
- 100g mushrooms, sliced
- 50g fresh spinach, chopped
- 50g shredded cheddar cheese
- Salt and black pepper, to taste

**Preparation instructions:**
1. Preheat the Air Fryer to 180°C for 5 minutes.
2. In a bowl, whisk together eggs, milk, salt, and pepper.
3. Grease the air fryer basket lightly.
4. Place mushrooms and spinach into the basket.
5. Pour the egg mixture over the mushrooms and spinach.
6. Sprinkle shredded cheddar cheese on top.
7. Air fry at 180°C for about 8 minutes or until the omelette is set and the cheese is melted.
8. Carefully remove from the air fryer, fold the omelette, and serve hot.

## Apple Cinnamon Breakfast Pastries

Makes: 4 pastries
Prep time: 15 minutes / Cook time: 10 minutes

**Ingredients:**
- 1 sheet ready-to-roll puff pastry (about 320g)
- 2 apples, peeled, cored, and thinly sliced
- 2 tbsp granulated sugar
- 1 tsp ground cinnamon
- 1 egg, beaten (for egg wash)

**Preparation instructions:**
1. Preheat the Air Fryer to 180°C for 5 minutes.
2. Cut the puff pastry into 4 squares.
3. In a bowl, toss apple slices with sugar and cinnamon.
4. Place apple slices onto each puff pastry square.
5. Fold the pastry over the apples, creating a pocket, and seal the edges with a fork.
6. Brush each pastry with beaten egg.
7. Place the pastries in the air fryer basket.

8. Air fry at 180°C for about 10 minutes or until the pastries are golden brown.
9. Remove from the air fryer and let cool slightly before serving.

## English Breakfast Potato Rosti

Serves: 4
Prep time: 15 minutes / Cook time: 15 minutes

**Ingredients:**
- 500g potatoes, peeled and grated
- 1 small onion, grated
- 2 tbsp olive oil
- Salt and black pepper, to taste

**Preparation instructions:**
1. Preheat the Air Fryer to 190°C for 5 minutes.
2. In a bowl, mix grated potatoes, grated onion, salt, and pepper.
3. Divide the mixture into 4 portions and shape them into flat rounds.
4. Brush both sides of each round with olive oil.
5. Place the potato rosti rounds in the air fryer basket.
6. Air fry at 190°C for about 15 minutes or until crispy and golden brown.
7. Remove from the air fryer and serve hot.

## Maple Glazed Breakfast Sausages

Serves: 4
Prep time: 5 minutes / Cook time: 10 minutes

**Ingredients:**
- 8 breakfast sausages
- 60ml maple syrup
- 1 tbsp olive oil

**Preparation instructions:**
1. Preheat the Air Fryer to 180°C for 5 minutes.
2. In a bowl, mix sausages with maple syrup and olive oil.
3. Place the sausages in the air fryer basket.
4. Air fry at 180°C for about 10 minutes, turning halfway through, until browned and cooked through.
5. Remove from the air fryer and let cool slightly before serving.

## Crispy Baked Avocado Toast

Serves: 2
Prep time: 5 minutes / Cook time: 6 minutes

**Ingredients:**
- 2 slices whole grain bread
- 1 ripe avocado, sliced
- 1 egg
- 30g shredded cheddar cheese
- Salt and black pepper, to taste

**Preparation instructions:**
1. Preheat the Air Fryer to 180°C for 5 minutes.
2. Place bread slices in the air fryer basket.
3. Air fry at 180°C for 2 minutes to lightly toast the bread.
4. Remove the bread from the air fryer.
5. Top each slice with avocado slices and sprinkle with salt and pepper.
6. Crack an egg onto each avocado toast.
7. Sprinkle shredded cheddar cheese on top of each egg.
8. Place the avocado toasts back in the air fryer basket.
9. Air fry at 180°C for about 4 minutes or until the eggs are cooked to your desired doneness.
10. Remove from the air fryer and serve hot.

## Banana-Stuffed French Toast Pockets

Serves: 2
Prep time: 10 minutes / Cook time: 8 minutes

**Ingredients:**
- 4 slices of bread, crusts removed
- 1 ripe banana, mashed
- 60ml whole milk
- 1 large egg
- 1 tbsp granulated sugar
- 1/2 tsp ground cinnamon
- 1/4 tsp vanilla extract
- Cooking spray or oil, for greasing

**Preparation instructions:**
1. Preheat the Air Fryer to 180°C for 5 minutes.
2. In a bowl, mix mashed banana, milk, egg, sugar, cinnamon, and vanilla extract.
3. Flatten the bread slices with a rolling pin.
4. Spread the banana mixture onto 2 slices of bread and cover each with the remaining slices,

creating 2 sandwiches.
5. Cut each sandwich into 2 pockets.
6. Lightly grease the air fryer basket with cooking spray or oil.
7. Place the stuffed pockets in the basket.
8. Air fry at 180°C for about 8 minutes, turning halfway through, until golden brown and crispy.
9. Remove from the air fryer and serve warm.

## Savory Spinach and Feta Breakfast Wraps

Serves: 2
Prep time: 10 minutes / Cook time: 6 minutes

**Ingredients:**
- 2 large tortilla wraps
- 100g fresh spinach leaves
- 50g feta cheese, crumbled
- 4 large eggs
- 60ml whole milk
- Salt and black pepper, to taste

**Preparation instructions:**
1. Preheat the Air Fryer to 180°C for 5 minutes.
2. Place spinach leaves evenly on each tortilla.
3. Sprinkle crumbled feta cheese over the spinach.
4. In a bowl, whisk together eggs, milk, salt, and pepper.
5. Pour half of the egg mixture over each tortilla.
6. Roll up the tortillas, tucking in the edges to create wraps.
7. Place the wraps in the air fryer basket.
8. Air fry at 180°C for about 6 minutes or until the egg is set and the wraps are lightly golden.
9. Remove from the air fryer and let cool slightly before serving.

## Air Fryer Breakfast Pizza

Serves: 2
Prep time: 10 minutes / Cook time: 10 minutes

**Ingredients:**
- 2 small tortilla wraps
- 4 tbsp tomato sauce or passata
- 50g shredded mozzarella cheese
- 4 slices cooked bacon, chopped
- 2 large eggs
- Salt and black pepper, to taste
- Chopped fresh herbs (optional)

**Preparation instructions:**
1. Preheat the Air Fryer to 180°C for 5 minutes.
2. Place tortilla wraps on a clean surface.
3. Spread tomato sauce over each wrap.
4. Sprinkle shredded mozzarella cheese evenly on top.
5. Add chopped bacon on the cheese.
6. Crack an egg onto the center of each pizza.
7. Season with salt and pepper.
8. Place the pizzas in the air fryer basket.
9. Air fry at 180°C for about 10 minutes or until the egg is cooked to your desired doneness and the edges are crispy.
10. Remove from the air fryer, garnish with fresh herbs if desired, and serve hot.

## Cinnamon Sugar Donut Holes

Makes: 12 donut holes
Prep time: 15 minutes / Cook time: 6 minutes

**Ingredients:**
- 150g plain flour
- 50g granulated sugar
- 1 tsp baking powder
- 1/4 tsp ground cinnamon
- 60ml whole milk
- 1 large egg
- 30g unsalted butter, melted
- Cooking spray or oil, for greasing
- 50g granulated sugar + 1 tsp ground cinnamon (for coating)

**Preparation instructions:**
1. Preheat the Air Fryer to 180°C for 5 minutes.
2. In a bowl, mix flour, sugar, baking powder, and cinnamon.
3. In another bowl, whisk together milk, egg, and melted butter.
4. Combine wet and dry Ingredients:, stirring until just combined.
5. Grease your hands and shape the dough into small balls (about 12).
6. Lightly grease the air fryer basket with cooking spray or oil.
7. Place the dough balls in the basket, ensuring they're not touching.
8. Air fry at 180°C for about 6 minutes, until golden brown.
9. In a separate bowl, mix sugar and cinnamon

for coating.
10. While still warm, roll the donut holes in the cinnamon sugar mixture until coated.
11. Let cool slightly and serve.

## Mediterranean Style Shakshuka

Serves: 2
Prep time: 10 minutes / Cook time: 12 minutes

**Ingredients:**
- 1 tbsp olive oil
- 1 small onion, finely chopped
- 2 cloves garlic, minced
- 1 red bell pepper, diced
- 400g canned chopped tomatoes
- 1 tsp paprika
- 1/2 tsp ground cumin
- 1/4 tsp cayenne pepper (optional)
- 4 large eggs
- Salt and black pepper, to taste
- Chopped fresh parsley (for garnish)

**Preparation instructions:**
1. Preheat the Air Fryer to 180°C for 5 minutes.
2. Heat olive oil in a skillet (oven-proof if transferring to air fryer).
3. Add chopped onion and sauté until translucent.
4. Stir in minced garlic and diced red bell pepper, cooking for another 2 minutes.
5. Add canned chopped tomatoes, paprika, ground cumin, and cayenne pepper (if using). Cook for 5 minutes until the sauce thickens slightly.
6. Transfer the tomato mixture to an oven-proof dish suitable for the air fryer if your skillet isn't air fryer safe.
7. Make small wells in the tomato mixture and crack an egg into each well.
8. Season with salt and pepper.
9. Place the dish in the air fryer basket.
10. Air fry at 180°C for about 12 minutes or until the egg whites are set but the yolks are still slightly runny.
11. Remove from the air fryer, garnish with chopped fresh parsley, and serve hot.

## Parmesan Crusted Breakfast Potatoes

Serves: 4
Prep time: 10 minutes / Cook time: 20 minutes

**Ingredients:**
- 600g potatoes, peeled and diced
- 2 tbsp olive oil
- 50g grated Parmesan cheese
- 1 tsp garlic powder
- 1 tsp dried thyme
- Salt and black pepper, to taste

**Preparation instructions:**
1. Preheat the Air Fryer to 200°C for 5 minutes.
2. In a bowl, toss diced potatoes with olive oil, Parmesan cheese, garlic powder, dried thyme, salt, and pepper until evenly coated.
3. Place the seasoned potatoes in the air fryer basket.
4. Air fry at 200°C for about 20 minutes, shaking the basket occasionally, until the potatoes are golden and crispy.
5. Remove from the air fryer and serve hot.

## Raspberry Cream Cheese Stuffed French Toast

Serves: 2
Prep time: 15 minutes / Cook time: 10 minutes

**Ingredients:**
- 4 slices thick bread
- 60g cream cheese
- 50g fresh raspberries, mashed
- 2 large eggs
- 60ml whole milk
- 1 tbsp granulated sugar
- 1/2 tsp vanilla extract
- Cooking spray or oil, for greasing

**Preparation instructions:**
1. Preheat the Air Fryer to 180°C for 5 minutes.
2. In a bowl, mix cream cheese and mashed raspberries until well combined.
3. Spread the cream cheese and raspberry mixture onto 2 slices of bread and cover each with the

remaining slices, creating 2 sandwiches.
4. In another bowl, whisk together eggs, milk, sugar, and vanilla extract.
5. Dip each sandwich into the egg mixture, coating both sides.
6. Lightly grease the air fryer basket with cooking spray or oil.
7. Place the sandwiches in the basket.
8. Air fry at 180°C for about 10 minutes, flipping halfway through, until golden brown and cooked through.
9. Remove from the air fryer, let cool slightly, and serve warm.

## Cheese and Ham Breakfast Quesadilla

Serves: 2
Prep time: 10 minutes / Cook time: 8 minutes

**Ingredients:**
- 2 large flour tortillas
- 100g grated cheddar cheese
- 4 slices ham
- 2 large eggs
- Salt and black pepper, to taste
- Cooking spray or oil, for greasing

**Preparation instructions:**
1. Preheat the Air Fryer to 180°C for 5 minutes.
2. Place one tortilla on a clean surface and sprinkle half of the grated cheese over half of the tortilla.
3. Layer ham slices over the cheese and fold the tortilla in half.
4. Repeat with the second tortilla and remaining cheese and ham.
5. Lightly grease the air fryer basket with cooking spray or oil.
6. Place the folded tortillas in the basket.
7. Crack an egg onto the top of each folded tortilla.
8. Season eggs with salt and pepper.
9. Air fry at 180°C for about 8 minutes or until the tortillas are crispy and the eggs are cooked to your liking.
10. Remove from the air fryer and serve hot.

## Air Fryer Churro Waffles

Makes: 4 waffles
Prep time: 15 minutes / Cook time: 6 minutes

**Ingredients:**
- 200g plain flour
- 60g granulated sugar
- 1 tsp baking powder
- 1/2 tsp ground cinnamon
- 240ml whole milk
- 60ml vegetable oil
- 1 tsp vanilla extract
- Cooking spray or oil, for greasing
- Cinnamon sugar mixture (1:1 ratio), for coating

**Preparation instructions:**
1. Preheat the Air Fryer to 200°C for 5 minutes.
2. In a bowl, whisk together flour, sugar, baking powder, and ground cinnamon.
3. Stir in milk, vegetable oil, and vanilla extract until the batter is smooth.
4. Lightly grease the waffle iron with cooking spray or oil.
5. Pour batter into the waffle iron and cook according to the manufacturer's instructions until golden and crisp.
6. Once cooked, remove the waffles and immediately coat them in the cinnamon sugar mixture.
7. Place the coated waffles in the air fryer basket.
8. Air fry at 200°C for about 6 minutes to crisp up the outer layer.
9. Remove from the air fryer and serve warm.

## English Muffin Breakfast Sandwiches

Serves: 2
Prep time: 10 minutes / Cook time: 8 minutes

**Ingredients:**
- 2 English muffins, split
- 4 large eggs
- 60ml whole milk
- Salt and black pepper, to taste
- 4 slices bacon or ham
- 50g grated cheddar cheese
- Cooking spray or oil, for greasing

**Preparation instructions:**
1. Preheat the Air Fryer to 180°C for 5 minutes.
2. Lightly grease the air fryer basket with cooking spray or oil.
3. Place English muffin halves in the basket, cut side up.

4. Crack an egg onto each muffin half.
5. Pour a little milk over each egg and season with salt and pepper.
6. Place bacon or ham slices on another rack or in a separate basket.
7. Air fry at 180°C for about 8 minutes or until the eggs are set and the bacon/ham is cooked to your liking.
8. Remove from the air fryer, sprinkle grated cheddar cheese over the eggs, and assemble the sandwiches using the bacon/ham and remaining English muffin halves.
9. Serve immediately while warm.

## Air Fryer Breakfast Tostadas Recipe

Prep time: 5 minutes
Cooking Time: 10-15 minutes / Serves: 4 people

**Ingredients:**
- 4 corn tortillas
- 300 g black beans, drained and rinsed
- 300 g shredded cheddar cheese
- 4 large eggs
- Salt and pepper, to taste
- Salsa, avocado, hot sauce, and cilantro, for serving (optional)

**Preparation instructions:**
1. Preheat the air fryer to 400°F (200°C).
2. Place the tortillas in a single layer in the air fryer basket. Then you can spray them with a butter flavoured cooking spray.
3. Cook the tortillas for 2-3 minutes, or until crispy and lightly golden.
4. Remove the tortillas from the air fryer and set aside.
5. In a bowl, mash the black beans with a fork.
6. Spread a layer of mashed black beans on each tortilla, followed by a sprinkle of shredded cheese.
7. In another bowl, whisk together the eggs, salt, and pepper.
8. Pour the egg mixture into the air fryer basket and cook for 5-7 minutes, or until fully cooked.
9. Place the cooked eggs on top of the cheese and black beans on each tortilla.
10. Return the tostadas to the air fryer and cook for an additional 2-3 minutes, or until the cheese is melted.
11. Serve the tostadas immediately with salsa, avocado, hot sauce, and cilantro, if desired.
12. Enjoy this tasty and easy air fryer breakfast tostada recipe!

## Air Fryer Cinnamon Sugar Churros

Prep time: 10 minutes
Cook Time: 10 minutes / Serves: 4

**Ingredients:**
- 1 cup (240 ml) water
- ½ cup (120 ml) unsalted butter
- 2 tbsp (25 g) granulated sugar
- ¼ tsp (1.25 ml) salt
- 1 cup (125 g) all-purpose flour
- 2 large eggs
- ¼ cup (50 g) granulated sugar
- 1 tsp (5 ml) ground cinnamon
- Cooking spray

**Preparation instructions:**
1. In a medium saucepan, combine water, unsalted butter, granulated sugar, and salt. Heat over medium heat until the butter has melted and the mixture comes to a boil.
2. Add the flour to the saucepan and stir until a dough forms. Remove the saucepan from the heat.
3. Add the eggs to the dough one at a time, stirring well after each addition. Continue stirring until the dough becomes smooth and shiny.
4. Preheat the air fryer to 200°C.
5. Coat the air fryer basket with cooking spray.
6. Fill a pastry bag with the churro dough.
7. Pipe the dough into 4-inch (10 cm) long strips in the air fryer basket, leaving enough space between them.
8. Cook for 6-8 minutes or until the churros are golden brown and crispy.
9. In a small bowl, mix the granulated sugar and ground cinnamon.
10. Once the churros are done, remove them from the air fryer basket and toss them in the cinnamon sugar mixture until they are coated evenly.
11. Serve immediately.

## Banana & Peanut butter Bagel

Serves 2
Prep time: 2 minutes / Cook time: 6 minutes

**Ingredients:**
- 2 cinnamon and raisin bagels
- 4 tsp olive margarine
- 2 tbsp crunchy peanut butter
- 2 large bananas

**Preparation instructions:**
1. Using a kitchen knife, cut the bagels horizontally to create 2 sliced halves
2. Spread 1 tsp of margarine on the inside of each sliced bagels
3. Place the bagels in the air fryer at 200°C for 6-7 minutes (crust layers facing down)
4. Meanwhile, peel and mash the bananas and set aside as 2 portions
5. Remove the bagels from the air fryer and put them on a plate (1 bagel per plate)
6. Inside each bagel, layer one side with 1 tbsp of peanut butter and the other side with mashed banana
7. Sandwich the bagel together and serve

## Air Fryer Breakfast Sweet Rolls

Serves: 2
Prep time: 15 minutes / Cook Time: 15 minutes

**Ingredients:**
- Pre-made sweet roll dough
- Unsalted butter, melted
- Brown sugar
- 1/2 tsp ground cinnamon
- Powdered sugar (for glaze)
- 1-2 tsp milk (for glaze)
- Optional toppings: chopped nuts, raisins, or dried fruits

**Preparation instructions:**
1. Preheat the Air Fryer to 175°C for 5 minutes.
2. Divide the pre-made sweet roll dough into 4 equal portions.
3. Roll each portion into a small ball and place them in the greased Air Fryer basket. Leave some space between each portion.
4. In a small bowl, mix together the melted butter, brown sugar, and ground cinnamon until well combined.
5. Drizzle the butter mixture over the sweet roll dough balls, ensuring each ball is coated evenly.
6. Place the basket in the Air Fryer and cook at 175°C for 12-15 minutes or until the sweet rolls are golden brown.
7. Once they turn golden brown, remove the sweet rolls from the Air Fryer and let them cool slightly.
8. In another small bowl, whisk together the powdered sugar and milk to make a glaze. Adjust the consistency with more milk if needed.
9. Drizzle the glaze over the warm sweet rolls and sprinkle with optional toppings if desired.
10. Serve the Air Fryer Breakfast Sweet Rolls while still warm and enjoy.

## Air Fryer Breakfast Tostadas Recipe

Prep time: 5 minutes
Cooking Time: 10-15 minutes / Serves: 4 people

**Ingredients:**
- 4 corn tortillas
- 300 g black beans, drained and rinsed
- 300 g shredded cheddar cheese
- 4 large eggs
- Salt and pepper, to taste
- Salsa, avocado, hot sauce, and cilantro, for serving (optional)

**Preparation instructions:**
1. Preheat the air fryer to 400°F (200°C).
2. Place the tortillas in a single layer in the air fryer basket. Then you can spray them with a butter flavoured cooking spray.
3. Cook the tortillas for 2-3 minutes, or until crispy and lightly golden.
4. Remove the tortillas from the air fryer and set aside.
5. In a bowl, mash the black beans with a fork.
6. Spread a layer of mashed black beans on each tortilla, followed by a sprinkle of shredded cheese.
7. In another bowl, whisk together the eggs, salt, and pepper.
8. Pour the egg mixture into the air fryer basket and cook for 5-7 minutes, or until fully cooked.
9. Place the cooked eggs on top of the cheese and black beans on each tortilla.

10. Return the tostadas to the air fryer and cook for an additional 2-3 minutes, or until the cheese is melted.
11. Serve the tostadas immediately with salsa, avocado, hot sauce, and cilantro, if desired.
12. Enjoy this tasty and easy air fryer breakfast tostada recipe!

# Traditional English Breakfast

Serves 2
Prep time: 10 minutes / Cook time: 20 minutes

**Ingredients:**
- 4 rashers of bacon
- 4 sausages
- 4 eggs
- 2 slices of black pudding
- 1 can of baked beans
- 2 tomatoes, halved
- 4 slices of bread, toasted
- Salt and pepper to taste

**Preparation instructions:**
1. Preheat the air fryer to 200°C.
2. Place the bacon, sausages, black pudding, and tomato halves on a baking sheet.
3. Roast in the oven for 10-15 minutes, flipping halfway through.
4. In a small saucepan, heat the baked beans over low heat.
5. Crack the eggs into a non-stick skillet and cook over medium heat until the whites are set and the yolks are still runny.
6. Season everything with salt and pepper to taste.
7. Serve the breakfast with the toasted bread, roasted tomatoes, beans, bacon, sausages, and eggs.

# Omelette

Serves: 1
Prep time: 5 mins Cook time: 8 - 10 mins

**Ingredients:**
- 3 eggs
- 2 tbsp milk
- Salt and pepper, to taste
- 30 g diced veggies (such as peppers, onions, and mushrooms)
- 25 g shredded cheese

**Preparation instructions:**
1. Preheat your air fryer to 180C.
2. In a small bowl, beat together the eggs, milk, salt, and pepper. Add the veggies and cheese to the bowl and mix well.
3. Pour the mixture into a small cake tin and put it in the air fryer basket and cook for 8-10 minutes, or until the omelette is cooked through and the edges are crispy.

# French Toast

Serves: 2
Prep time: 5 mins Cook time: 5- 7 mins

**Ingredients:**
- 2 eggs
- 120 ml milk
- 1 tsp vanilla extract
- 1/2 tsp cinnamon
- 4 slices bread
- Butter, for spreading

**Preparation instructions:**
1. Preheat your air fryer to 180C.
2. In a small bowl, whisk together the eggs, milk, vanilla extract, and cinnamon.
3. Dip each slice of bread into the egg mixture, making sure to coat both sides evenly.
4. Spread a thin layer of butter on one side of each slice of bread.
5. Place the bread in the air fryer basket, butter side down, and cook for 5-7 minutes, or until the French toast is golden brown.

# Chapter 2: Lunch

## Crispy Fish and Chips

Serves: 2
Prep time: 15 minutes / Cook time: 20 minutes

**Ingredients:**
- 2 fillets of white fish (about 300g), such as cod or haddock
- 50g plain flour
- 1 large egg, beaten
- 50g breadcrumbs
- 1/2 tsp paprika
- Salt and black pepper, to taste
- Cooking spray or oil, for greasing

**Preparation instructions:**
1. Preheat the Air Fryer to 200°C for 5 minutes.
2. Pat dry the fish fillets with paper towels.
3. Season the flour with paprika, salt, and pepper in a shallow bowl.
4. Dip each fish fillet in flour, then egg, and finally coat with breadcrumbs.
5. Lightly grease the air fryer basket with cooking spray or oil.
6. Place the coated fish fillets in the basket.
7. Air fry at 200°C for about 15-20 minutes or until the fish is crispy and cooked through, flipping halfway through for even cooking.
8. Serve hot with chips or your desired accompaniments.

## Spicy Chicken Tikka Skewers

Serves: 2
Prep time: 15 minutes / Cook time: 12 minutes

**Ingredients:**
- 300g chicken breast, cut into chunks
- 60g plain Greek yoghurt
- 2 tbsp tikka masala paste
- 1/2 tsp ground cumin
- 1/2 tsp ground coriander
- 1/4 tsp cayenne pepper (adjust to taste)
- Salt, to taste
- Cooking spray or oil, for greasing

**Preparation instructions:**
1. In a bowl, mix together Greek yoghurt, tikka masala paste, ground cumin, ground coriander, cayenne pepper, and salt.
2. Add chicken chunks to the marinade and coat well. Let it marinate for at least 10 minutes.
3. Preheat the Air Fryer to 180°C for 5 minutes.
4. Thread marinated chicken onto skewers.
5. Lightly grease the air fryer basket with cooking spray or oil.
6. Place the chicken skewers in the basket.
7. Air fry at 180°C for about 10-12 minutes or until the chicken is cooked through, turning once halfway through for even cooking.
8. Serve hot with a side salad or rice.

## Mediterranean Stuffed Bell Peppers

Serves: 4
Prep time: 20 minutes / Cook time: 20 minutes

**Ingredients:**
- 4 bell peppers (any colour), halved and seeds removed
- 200g cooked quinoa or couscous
- 100g cherry tomatoes, chopped
- 50g feta cheese, crumbled
- 50g black olives, sliced
- 2 tbsp chopped fresh parsley
- 1 tbsp olive oil
- Salt and black pepper, to taste

**Preparation instructions:**
1. Preheat the Air Fryer to 180°C for 5 minutes.
2. In a bowl, mix together cooked quinoa or couscous, cherry tomatoes, feta cheese, black olives, chopped parsley, olive oil, salt, and pepper.
3. Stuff each bell pepper half with the mixture.
4. Lightly grease the air fryer basket with cooking spray or oil.
5. Place the stuffed bell peppers in the basket.
6. Air fry at 180°C for about 18-20 minutes or until the peppers are tender.
7. Serve hot as a side dish or main course.

## Air Fried Veggie Quesadillas

Serves: 2
Prep time: 10 minutes / Cook time: 10 minutes

**Ingredients:**
- 4 large flour tortillas
- 100g grated cheese (cheddar, mozzarella, or a blend)
- 1 bell pepper, thinly sliced
- 1 small red onion, thinly sliced
- 1 medium tomato, thinly sliced
- Cooking spray or oil, for greasing

**Preparation instructions:**
1. Preheat the Air Fryer to 180°C for 5 minutes.
2. Place a tortilla on a clean surface.
3. Spread a layer of grated cheese on half of the tortilla.
4. Add sliced bell pepper, red onion, and tomato over the cheese.
5. Fold the tortilla in half, pressing gently to seal.
6. Lightly grease the air fryer basket with cooking spray or oil.
7. Place the quesadilla in the basket.
8. Air fry at 180°C for about 5 minutes, flip, and continue cooking for another 5 minutes or until golden and crispy.
9. Repeat the process for the remaining quesadillas if needed.
10. Serve hot, cut into wedges, with salsa or sour cream if desired.

## Pesto Chicken Panini Melts

Serves: 2
Prep time: 15 minutes / Cook time: 8 minutes

**Ingredients:**
- 2 boneless, skinless chicken breasts (about 300g)
- 4 slices bread of your choice
- 4 tbsp pesto sauce
- 100g sliced mozzarella cheese
- Cooking spray or oil, for greasing

**Preparation instructions:**
1. Preheat the Air Fryer to 200°C for 5 minutes.
2. Season chicken breasts with salt and pepper.
3. Air fry the chicken breasts at 200°C for about 8-10 minutes or until cooked through, then slice into strips.
4. Spread pesto sauce on two slices of bread each.
5. Place cooked chicken strips on top of the pesto sauce.
6. Add mozzarella cheese slices over the chicken.
7. Top with the remaining slices of bread to form sandwiches.
8. Lightly grease the air fryer basket with cooking spray or oil.
9. Place the sandwiches in the basket.
10. Air fry at 180°C for about 5 minutes or until the bread is toasted and the cheese is melted.
11. Remove from the air fryer, slice diagonally, and serve hot.

## Crunchy Falafel Balls

Serves: 4
Prep time: 15 minutes / Cook time: 15 minutes

**Ingredients:**
- 400g canned chickpeas, drained and rinsed
- 1 small onion, finely chopped
- 2 cloves garlic, minced
- 2 tbsp chopped fresh parsley
- 1 tsp ground cumin
- 1 tsp ground coriander
- 1/2 tsp baking powder
- 2 tbsp plain flour
- Salt and black pepper, to taste
- Cooking spray or oil, for greasing

**Preparation instructions:**
1. Preheat the Air Fryer to 180°C for 5 minutes.
2. In a food processor, combine chickpeas, onion, garlic, parsley, cumin, coriander, baking powder, flour, salt, and pepper. Pulse until a coarse mixture forms.
3. Shape the mixture into small balls.
4. Lightly grease the air fryer basket with cooking spray or oil.
5. Place the falafel balls in the basket.
6. Air fry at 180°C for about 12-15 minutes or until golden brown and crispy, shaking or turning halfway through for even cooking.
7. Remove from the air fryer and serve hot with your favorite dipping sauce or in pita pockets.

## Air Fryer Beef and Vegetable Kebabs

Serves: 4
Prep time: 20 minutes / Cook time: 12 minutes

**Ingredients:**
- 400g beef steak, cut into cubes
- 1 red bell pepper, cut into chunks
- 1 green bell pepper, cut into chunks
- 1 red onion, cut into chunks
- 2 tbsp olive oil
- 2 cloves garlic, minced
- 1 tsp paprika
- 1 tsp ground cumin
- 1/2 tsp ground black pepper
- Salt, to taste
- Skewers (if using wooden skewers, soak them in water for 20 minutes before use)
- Cooking spray or oil, for greasing

**Preparation instructions:**
1. Preheat the Air Fryer to 200°C for 5 minutes.
2. In a bowl, combine beef cubes, bell peppers, red onion, olive oil, minced garlic, paprika, cumin, black pepper, and salt. Toss until well coated.
3. Thread the marinated beef and vegetable chunks onto skewers.
4. Lightly grease the air fryer basket with cooking spray or oil.
5. Place the skewers in the basket.
6. Air fry at 200°C for about 10-12 minutes, turning halfway through, until the beef is cooked to your desired doneness and the vegetables are tender.
7. Remove from the air fryer and serve hot, optionally with a side of rice or salad.

## Sticky Teriyaki Tofu

Serves: 2
Prep time: 15 minutes / Cook time: 15 minutes

**Ingredients:**
- 300g firm tofu, pressed and cut into cubes
- 60ml teriyaki sauce
- 1 tbsp honey or maple syrup
- 1 tbsp soy sauce
- 1 tbsp rice vinegar
- 1 clove garlic, minced
- 1 tsp sesame seeds (optional)
- Cooking spray or oil, for greasing

**Preparation instructions:**
1. Preheat the Air Fryer to 180°C for 5 minutes.
2. In a bowl, mix teriyaki sauce, honey or maple syrup, soy sauce, rice vinegar, minced garlic, and sesame seeds (if using).
3. Add tofu cubes to the mixture and toss to coat evenly.
4. Lightly grease the air fryer basket with cooking spray or oil.
5. Place the marinated tofu cubes in the basket, reserving the remaining marinade.
6. Air fry at 180°C for about 12-15 minutes or until the tofu is golden and slightly crispy, brushing with the reserved marinade halfway through.
7. Remove from the air fryer and serve hot, garnished with sesame seeds if desired.

## Cheese and Bacon Stuffed Mushrooms

Serves: 4
Prep time: 15 minutes / Cook time: 12 minutes

**Ingredients:**
- 8 large button mushrooms, stems removed and cleaned
- 50g cream cheese
- 50g grated cheddar cheese
- 2 slices bacon, cooked and crumbled
- 1 tbsp chopped fresh parsley
- Salt and black pepper, to taste
- Cooking spray or oil, for greasing

**Preparation instructions:**
1. Preheat the Air Fryer to 180°C for 5 minutes.
2. In a bowl, mix together cream cheese, grated cheddar cheese, crumbled bacon, chopped parsley, salt, and pepper.
3. Stuff each mushroom cap with the cheese and bacon mixture.
4. Lightly grease the air fryer basket with cooking spray or oil.
5. Place the stuffed mushrooms in the basket.
6. Air fry at 180°C for about 10-12 minutes or until the mushrooms are cooked through and the filling is golden and bubbly.
7. Remove from the air fryer and serve hot as a

delicious appetizer or side dish.

## Sweet Potato and Chickpea Patties

Serves: 4
Prep time: 20 minutes / Cook time: 15 minutes

**Ingredients:**
- 300g sweet potatoes, boiled and mashed
- 200g canned chickpeas, drained and mashed
- 1 small onion, finely chopped
- 2 cloves garlic, minced
- 2 tbsp chopped fresh coriander
- 1 tsp ground cumin
- 1 tsp ground coriander
- 1/2 tsp smoked paprika
- Salt and black pepper, to taste
- 50g breadcrumbs
- Cooking spray or oil, for greasing

**Preparation instructions:**
1. Preheat the Air Fryer to 190°C for 5 minutes.
2. In a bowl, combine mashed sweet potatoes, mashed chickpeas, chopped onion, minced garlic, chopped coriander, ground cumin, ground coriander, smoked paprika, salt, and pepper.
3. Form the mixture into patties.
4. Coat each patty with breadcrumbs.
5. Lightly grease the air fryer basket with cooking spray or oil.
6. Place the patties in the basket.
7. Air fry at 190°C for about 12-15 minutes or until the patties are golden and crispy, flipping halfway through for even cooking.
8. Remove from the air fryer and serve hot as a vegetarian main dish or in sandwiches.

## Air Fryer Chicken Caesar Wraps

Serves: 2
Prep time: 15 minutes / Cook time: 12 minutes

**Ingredients:**
- 2 boneless, skinless chicken breasts (about 300g)
- 2 tbsp olive oil
- 1 tsp garlic powder
- 1 tsp dried oregano
- Salt and black pepper, to taste
- 2 large flour tortillas
- 100g romaine lettuce, chopped
- 50g grated Parmesan cheese
- 4 tbsp Caesar dressing

**Preparation instructions:**
1. Preheat the Air Fryer to 180°C for 5 minutes.
2. Rub chicken breasts with olive oil, garlic powder, dried oregano, salt, and pepper.
3. Place the seasoned chicken breasts in the air fryer basket.
4. Air fry at 180°C for about 10-12 minutes or until the chicken is cooked through.
5. Remove the chicken from the air fryer, let it cool slightly, and slice into strips.
6. Warm the tortillas in the air fryer for 1-2 minutes.
7. Lay out the tortillas and divide the chopped lettuce equally onto each.
8. Add sliced chicken, grated Parmesan cheese, and drizzle with Caesar dressing.
9. Roll up the tortillas, folding in the sides, to form wraps.
10. Optionally, lightly spray the wraps with cooking spray and place them in the air fryer for an additional 2-3 minutes to crisp up the edges.
11. Serve the chicken Caesar wraps immediately.

## Pork and Apple Sausage Rolls

Makes: 6 rolls
Prep time: 20 minutes / Cook time: 15 minutes

**Ingredients:**
- 300g pork sausage meat
- 1 apple, peeled and finely grated
- 1 tbsp fresh sage, finely chopped
- 1/2 tsp ground nutmeg
- Salt and black pepper, to taste
- 320g puff pastry, rolled out
- 1 egg, beaten (for egg wash)

**Preparation instructions:**
1. Preheat the Air Fryer to 180°C for 5 minutes.
2. In a bowl, mix together pork sausage meat, grated apple, chopped sage, ground nutmeg, salt, and pepper.
3. Cut the puff pastry into 6 rectangles.
4. Divide the sausage mixture into 6 portions and shape them into logs.
5. Place each sausage log onto a puff pastry rectangle, then roll the pastry around the

sausage and seal the edges.
6. Brush the sausage rolls with beaten egg for an egg wash.
7. Place the sausage rolls in the air fryer basket, leaving space between each roll.
8. Air fry at 180°C for about 12-15 minutes or until the rolls are golden and cooked through.
9. Remove from the air fryer and allow to cool slightly before serving.

## Tex-Mex Loaded Nachos

Serves: 4
Prep time: 10 minutes / Cook time: 8 minutes

**Ingredients:**
- 200g tortilla chips
- 200g shredded cheddar cheese
- 200g cooked black beans, drained
- 1 red onion, finely chopped
- 1 tomato, diced
- 1 jalapeño, sliced
- 1 avocado, diced
- Fresh coriander leaves, chopped (optional)
- Sour cream and salsa, for serving

**Preparation instructions:**
1. Preheat the Air Fryer to 180°C for 5 minutes.
2. Spread the tortilla chips evenly in the air fryer basket.
3. Sprinkle shredded cheddar cheese and cooked black beans over the chips.
4. Air fry at 180°C for about 5-8 minutes or until the cheese is melted and bubbly.
5. Remove the nachos from the air fryer and transfer to a serving plate.
6. Top with chopped red onion, diced tomato, sliced jalapeño, diced avocado, and chopped fresh coriander leaves (if using).
7. Serve immediately with sour cream and salsa on the side.

## Air Fryer Caprese Stuffed Chicken Breast

Serves: 2
Prep time: 15 minutes / Cook time: 20 minutes

**Ingredients:**
- 2 chicken breasts (about 300g)
- 4 slices mozzarella cheese
- 2 large tomatoes, sliced
- Fresh basil leaves
- Salt and black pepper, to taste
- 2 tbsp balsamic glaze
- Cooking spray or oil, for greasing

**Preparation instructions:**
1. Preheat the Air Fryer to 200°C for 5 minutes.
2. Make a horizontal slit in each chicken breast to create a pocket.
3. Season the chicken breasts with salt and pepper.
4. Stuff each chicken breast with slices of mozzarella, tomato, and fresh basil leaves.
5. Secure the chicken breasts with toothpicks to hold the filling.
6. Lightly grease the air fryer basket with cooking spray or oil.
7. Place the stuffed chicken breasts in the basket.
8. Air fry at 200°C for about 18-20 minutes or until the chicken is thoroughly cooked.
9. Drizzle balsamic glaze over the stuffed chicken breasts before serving.
10. Remove the toothpicks, slice, and serve hot.

## Crispy Coconut Shrimp

Serves: 4
Prep time: 20 minutes / Cook time: 10 minutes

**Ingredients:**
- 400g large shrimp, peeled and deveined
- 100g desiccated coconut
- 50g breadcrumbs
- 2 eggs, beaten
- Salt and black pepper, to taste
- Cooking spray or oil, for greasing

**Preparation instructions:**
1. Preheat the Air Fryer to 200°C for 5 minutes.
2. Pat dry the shrimp with paper towels and season with salt and pepper.
3. In separate bowls, place beaten eggs, desiccated coconut, and breadcrumbs.
4. Dip each shrimp in the beaten eggs, then coat with coconut and breadcrumb mixture.
5. Lightly grease the air fryer basket with cooking spray or oil.
6. Place the coated shrimp in the basket, leaving space between each shrimp.
7. Air fry at 200°C for about 5-6 minutes, flip the

shrimp, and air fry for another 4-5 minutes or until golden and crispy.
8. Remove from the air fryer and serve hot with your preferred dipping sauce.

## Air Fried Falafel Wraps

Serves: 2
Prep time: 20 minutes / Cook time: 15 minutes

**Ingredients:**
- 200g canned chickpeas, drained and rinsed
- 1 small onion, finely chopped
- 2 cloves garlic, minced
- 2 tbsp chopped fresh parsley
- 1 tsp ground cumin
- 1 tsp ground coriander
- 1/2 tsp baking powder
- Salt and black pepper, to taste
- Cooking spray or oil, for greasing
- 2 large tortilla wraps
- Hummus, lettuce, tomatoes, cucumber (for serving)

**Preparation instructions:**
1. Preheat the Air Fryer to 180°C for 5 minutes.
2. In a food processor, blend chickpeas, onion, garlic, parsley, cumin, coriander, baking powder, salt, and pepper until it forms a coarse mixture.
3. Shape the mixture into small balls and slightly flatten them into patties.
4. Lightly grease the air fryer basket with cooking spray or oil.
5. Place the falafel patties in the basket, leaving space between each one.
6. Air fry at 180°C for about 12-15 minutes or until the falafel is crispy and golden brown, flipping halfway through for even cooking.
7. Warm the tortilla wraps in the air fryer for 1-2 minutes.
8. Spread hummus on the wraps, add lettuce, tomatoes, cucumber, and place the air-fried falafel inside.
9. Roll up the wraps and serve immediately.

## Spinach and Feta Stuffed Portobello Mushrooms

Serves: 2
Prep time: 15 minutes / Cook time: 12 minutes

**Ingredients:**
- 4 large Portobello mushrooms
- 100g fresh spinach, chopped
- 50g feta cheese, crumbled
- 2 cloves garlic, minced
- 1 tbsp olive oil
- Salt and black pepper, to taste
- Cooking spray or oil, for greasing

**Preparation instructions:**
1. Preheat the Air Fryer to 180°C for 5 minutes.
2. Remove the stems from the Portobello mushrooms and scrape out the gills.
3. In a pan, heat olive oil over medium heat and sauté minced garlic until fragrant.
4. Add chopped spinach to the pan and cook until wilted.
5. Remove the pan from heat and stir in crumbled feta cheese, salt, and pepper.
6. Fill each Portobello mushroom with the spinach and feta mixture.
7. Lightly grease the air fryer basket with cooking spray or oil.
8. Place the stuffed mushrooms in the basket.
9. Air fry at 180°C for about 10-12 minutes or until the mushrooms are tender and the filling is golden on top.
10. Remove from the air fryer and serve hot.

## Sticky Hoisin Glazed Salmon

Serves: 2
Prep time: 10 minutes / Cook time: 10 minutes

**Ingredients:**
- 2 salmon fillets (about 200g each)
- 2 tbsp hoisin sauce
- 1 tbsp soy sauce
- 1 tbsp honey
- 1 tsp sesame oil
- 1 tsp minced ginger
- 1 garlic clove, minced
- Sesame seeds and chopped spring onions (for garnish)
- Cooking spray or oil, for greasing

**Preparation instructions:**
1. Preheat the Air Fryer to 200°C for 5 minutes.
2. In a bowl, mix hoisin sauce, soy sauce, honey, sesame oil, minced ginger, and minced garlic.
3. Brush the salmon fillets with the prepared glaze

on both sides.
4. Lightly grease the air fryer basket with cooking spray or oil.
5. Place the salmon fillets in the basket.
6. Air fry at 200°C for about 8-10 minutes or until the salmon is cooked through and glaze is caramelized.
7. Garnish with sesame seeds and chopped spring onions before serving.

## Air Fryer BBQ Pork Ribs

Serves: 2
Prep time: 15 minutes / Cook time: 40 minutes

**Ingredients:**
- 500g pork ribs
- 150ml BBQ sauce
- 2 tbsp soy sauce
- 1 tbsp brown sugar
- 1 tbsp apple cider vinegar
- 1 tsp smoked paprika
- 1/2 tsp garlic powder
- 1/2 tsp onion powder
- Salt and black pepper, to taste

**Preparation instructions:**
1. Preheat the Air Fryer to 180°C for 5 minutes.
2. In a bowl, mix BBQ sauce, soy sauce, brown sugar, apple cider vinegar, smoked paprika, garlic powder, onion powder, salt, and pepper.
3. Rub the pork ribs with the prepared BBQ sauce mixture, covering them evenly.
4. Place the ribs in the air fryer basket.
5. Air fry at 180°C for about 35-40 minutes, turning halfway through and brushing with additional sauce if desired, until the ribs are cooked and tender.
6. Remove from the air fryer and let rest for a few minutes before serving.

## Cheesy Broccoli Bites

Makes: 12 bites
Prep time: 15 minutes / Cook time: 10 minutes

**Ingredients:**
- 300g broccoli florets, steamed and chopped
- 100g breadcrumbs
- 100g grated cheddar cheese
- 2 eggs, beaten
- 1 garlic clove, minced
- Salt and black pepper, to taste
- Cooking spray or oil, for greasing

**Preparation instructions:**
1. Preheat the Air Fryer to 180°C for 5 minutes.
2. In a bowl, combine chopped broccoli, breadcrumbs, grated cheddar cheese, beaten eggs, minced garlic, salt, and pepper.
3. Shape the mixture into small bites or patties.
4. Lightly grease the air fryer basket with cooking spray or oil.
5. Place the broccoli bites in the basket.
6. Air fry at 180°C for about 8-10 minutes or until the bites are golden and crispy.
7. Remove from the air fryer and serve warm as a delicious snack or side dish.

## Chicken Biryani

Serves: 4-6 servings
Prep time: 20 minutes / Cook time: 40 minutes

**Ingredients:**
- 500g chicken thighs, bone-in, skinless, cut into pieces
- 400g basmati rice, rinsed and soaked for 30 minutes
- 2 onions, thinly sliced
- 2 tomatoes, chopped
- 4 cloves garlic, minced
- 1-inch piece of ginger, grated
- 2 green chillies, slit lengthwise (adjust according to spice preference)
- 1 teaspoon turmeric powder
- 1 teaspoon red chilli powder
- 1 teaspoon cumin powder
- 1 teaspoon coriander powder
- 1 teaspoon garam masala
- 120g plain yoghourt
- 15g chopped fresh cilantro
- 10g chopped fresh mint leaves
- 960g chicken broth
- 4 tablespoons ghee (clarified butter) or vegetable oil
- Salt to taste

**Preparation instructions:**
1. In a large skillet or pot, heat the ghee or vegetable oil over medium heat. Add the sliced onions and cook until they turn golden brown and caramelised. Remove half of the onions and set them aside for garnishing.

2. To the remaining onions in the skillet, add the minced garlic, grated ginger, and green chillies. Sauté for 1-2 minutes until fragrant.
3. Add the chicken pieces to the skillet and cook until they are browned on all sides.
4. Stir in the chopped tomatoes, turmeric powder, red chilli powder, cumin powder, coriander powder, and salt. Cook for 2-3 minutes until the tomatoes soften.
5. Add the plain yoghourt, chopped cilantro, and chopped mint leaves. Mix well to coat the chicken with the spices.
6. Drain the soaked basmati rice and add it to the skillet. Stir gently to combine everything.
7. Pour in the chicken broth and bring the mixture to a boil. Once boiling, reduce the heat to low, cover the skillet, and let it simmer for about 20-25 minutes or until the rice is cooked and the chicken is tender.
8. Once cooked, remove from heat and let it rest for a few minutes.
9. Fluff the biryani gently with a fork and garnish with the reserved caramelised onions.
10. Serve the flavourful chicken biryani hot with raita (yoghourt sauce) or a side salad.

# Air Fryer Buffalo Chicken Wings

Serves 4
Prep time: 10 minutes / Cook time: 25-30 minutes

**Ingredients:**
- 900 g chicken wings
- 60 ml hot sauce
- 60 ml melted butter
- 1 tsp. garlic powder
- 1 tsp. salt
- 1/2 tsp. black pepper

**Preparation instructions:**
1. Preheat air fryer to 190°C.
2. Pat chicken wings dry with paper towels.
3. In a large bowl, whisk together hot sauce, melted butter, garlic powder, salt, and black pepper.
4. Toss chicken wings in sauce mixture until evenly coated.
5. Place chicken wings in air fryer basket in a single layer, making sure they are not touching.
6. Cook for 25-30 minutes, flipping halfway through, until chicken is cooked through and crispy.

# Air Fryer Chicken Tikka Skewers

Serves 4
Prep Time 15 minutes / Cook Time 15 minutes

**Ingredients:**
- 500g boneless chicken breasts, cut into chunks
- 200g Greek yogurt
- 2 tablespoons tikka masala paste
- 1 red bell pepper, cut into chunks
- 1 onion, cut into chunks

**Preparation instructions:**
1. In a large bowl, mix together the Greek yoghourt and tikka masala paste.
2. Add the chicken and toss to coat. Marinate in the refrigerator for at least 2 hours.
3. Thread the marinated chicken, bell pepper, and onion onto skewers.
4. Place the skewers in the air fryer basket. Cook at 180°C for 15 minutes, turning halfway through, until the chicken is cooked through and the vegetables are tender.

# Air Fryer Duck Breast with Orange Glaze

Serves: 2
Cooking Time: 30 minutes

**Ingredients:**
- 2 duck breasts
- 2 tbsp honey
- Juice and zest of 1 orange
- 1 tbsp soy sauce
- 1 tsp garlic powder
- Salt and pepper to taste

**Preparation instructions:**
1. Preheat the air fryer to 200°C.
2. Score the skin of the duck breasts in a criss-cross pattern.
3. In a small bowl, whisk together the honey, orange juice and zest, soy sauce, garlic powder, salt and pepper.
4. Brush the glaze onto the duck breasts, making

sure to coat the skin side well.
5. Place the duck breasts skin-side down in the air fryer basket and cook for 15 minutes.
6. Flip the duck breasts and brush the skin with more glaze.
7. Cook for another 10-15 minutes, or until the internal temperature reaches 70°C.
8. Let the duck breasts rest for 5 minutes before slicing and serving.

## Honey Garlic Pork Chops

Serves 4,
Cooking Time: 20 minutes

**Ingredients:**
- 4 bone-in pork chops (each about 200g)
- 2 cloves garlic, minced
- 2 tablespoons honey
- 2 tablespoons soy sauce
- 1 tablespoon olive oil
- 1/2 teaspoon ground ginger
- Salt and pepper, to taste

**Preparation instructions:**
1. Preheat the air fryer to 200°C.
2. Pat the pork chops dry with paper towels and season with salt and pepper.
3. In a small bowl, whisk together the garlic, honey, soy sauce, olive oil, and ginger.
4. Brush the mixture over both sides of the pork chops.
5. Place the pork chops in the air fryer basket and cook for 10 minutes.
6. Flip the pork chops and cook for another 8-10 minutes, until the internal temperature reaches 63°C.
7. Remove the pork chops from the air fryer and let them rest for a few minutes before serving.

## Air Fryer BBQ Ribs

Serves: 4 people
Prep time: 10 minutes / Cooking Time: 45 minutes

**Ingredients:**
- 1 kg pork spare ribs
- 1 tsp garlic powder
- 1 tsp onion powder
- 1 tsp smoked paprika
- 1 tsp dried oregano
- 1 tsp dried thyme
- 1 tsp salt
- 1 tsp black pepper
- 200 ml barbecue sauce

**Preparation instructions:**
1. In a large bowl, mix together the garlic powder, onion powder, smoked paprika, oregano, thyme, salt, and black pepper.
2. Rub the mixture evenly over the spare ribs.
3. Place the seasoned ribs in the air fryer basket and cook at 180°C (360°F) for 15 minutes.
4. Flip the ribs over and cook for an additional 15 minutes.
5. Brush the barbecue sauce over the ribs, making sure to coat both sides.
6. Cook for another 10-15 minutes, or until the internal temperature of the ribs reaches 75°C (165°F).
7. Let the ribs rest for a few minutes before cutting and serving. Enjoy your delicious BBQ ribs in the air fryer!

## Air Fryer Bacon Wrapped Avocados

Serves: 4
Prep time: 10 minutes / Cook Time: 12 minutes

**Ingredients:**
- 2 ripe avocados, pitted and sliced into 8 wedges each
- 8 slices of bacon
- Salt and pepper, to taste
- ¼ tsp (1g) paprika
- ¼ tsp (1g) garlic powder

**Preparation instructions:**
1. Preheat your air fryer to 200°C.
2. Cut each slice of bacon in half lengthwise.
3. Wrap each avocado wedge with a half slice of bacon, securing it with a toothpick.
4. In a small bowl, combine the salt, pepper, paprika, and garlic powder.
5. Sprinkle the seasoning mixture over the bacon-wrapped avocado wedges.
6. Place the avocado wedges in the air fryer basket in a single layer.
7. Cook for 12 minutes or until the bacon is crispy, flipping the avocado wedges over halfway through the cooking time.
8. Once the avocado wedges are done, remove

them from the air fryer and let them cool slightly before serving. Remove the toothpicks from the avocado wedges before

## Kung Pao Chicken

Serves: 4
Prep time: 5 mins / Cook time: 8 -10 mins

**Ingredients:**
- 500g boneless, skinless chicken thighs, diced
- 2 tablespoons cornflour
- 2 tablespoons soy sauce
- 1 tablespoon rice vinegar
- 2 teaspoons sugar
- 1 teaspoon sesame oil
- 2 cloves of garlic, minced
- 1 teaspoon grated ginger
- 1/4 teaspoon red pepper flakes
- 2 tablespoons vegetable oil
- 1 red pepper, diced
- 30 g unsalted peanuts

**Preparation instructions:**
1. In a mixing bowl, combine the chicken, cornflour, soy sauce, rice vinegar, sugar, sesame oil, garlic, ginger, and red pepper flakes. Mix well.
2. Preheat your air fryer to 180C.
3. Place the chicken in a single layer in the air fryer and cook for 8-10 minutes or until cooked through.

## Honey Mustard Air Fryer Chicken Drumsticks

Serves 2
Prep time: 10 minutes / Cook time: 25 minutes

**Ingredients:**
- 4 chicken drumsticks
- 2 tablespoons Dijon mustard
- 2 tablespoons honey
- 1 tablespoon olive oil
- 1 teaspoon garlic powder
- 1/2 teaspoon paprika
- 1/2 teaspoon salt
- 1/4 teaspoon black pepper

**Preparation instructions:**
1. In a small bowl, whisk together the Dijon mustard, honey, olive oil, garlic powder, paprika, salt, and black pepper.
2. Brush the honey mustard mixture over the chicken drumsticks, ensuring they are well coated.
3. Place the chicken drumsticks in the air fryer basket, making sure they are not touching.
4. Warm up the air fryer to 200°C for 5 minutes before putting in the chicken.
5. Place the chicken drumsticks in the air fryer for 20-25 minutes, cooking at the same 200°C.
6. When finished cooking, take the chicken drumsticks out of the air fryer and set them aside to rest before serving.

# Chapter 3: Dinner

## Balsamic Glazed Air Fryer Pork Tenderloin

Serves: 4
Prep time: 10 minutes / Cook time: 20 minutes

**Ingredients:**
- 600g pork tenderloin
- 60ml balsamic vinegar
- 2 tbsp olive oil
- 2 cloves garlic, minced
- 1 tbsp honey
- 1 tsp dried thyme
- Salt and black pepper, to taste

**Preparation instructions:**
1. Preheat the Air Fryer to 200°C for 5 minutes.
2. In a bowl, mix balsamic vinegar, olive oil, minced garlic, honey, dried thyme, salt, and black pepper.
3. Coat the pork tenderloin with the prepared marinade.
4. Place the pork in the air fryer basket.
5. Air fry at 200°C for about 18-20 minutes, turning halfway through, until the internal temperature reaches 63°C.
6. Remove the pork from the air fryer, let it rest for a few minutes, then slice before serving.

## Air Fried Lemon Herb Chicken Thighs

Serves: 4
Prep time: 10 minutes / Cook time: 25 minutes

**Ingredients:**
- 8 chicken thighs, bone-in, skin-on
- Zest and juice of 1 lemon
- 2 tbsp olive oil
- 2 cloves garlic, minced
- 1 tsp dried mixed herbs (such as thyme, rosemary, oregano)
- Salt and black pepper, to taste

**Preparation instructions:**
1. Preheat the Air Fryer to 190°C for 5 minutes.
2. In a bowl, mix lemon zest, lemon juice, olive oil, minced garlic, dried mixed herbs, salt, and black pepper.
3. Pat dry the chicken thighs and coat them with the prepared marinade.
4. Place the chicken thighs in the air fryer basket.
5. Air fry at 190°C for about 22-25 minutes, turning once halfway through, until the chicken reaches an internal temperature of 75°C and the skin is crispy.
6. Serve the lemon herb chicken thighs hot.

## Crispy Coconut-Crusted Cod Fillets

Serves: 4
Prep time: 15 minutes / Cook time: 12 minutes

**Ingredients:**
- 4 cod fillets (about 150g each)
- 50g shredded coconut
- 50g breadcrumbs
- 1 egg, beaten
- 1 tbsp olive oil
- 1/2 tsp paprika
- Salt and black pepper, to taste

**Preparation instructions:**
1. Preheat the Air Fryer to 200°C for 5 minutes.
2. In a bowl, mix shredded coconut, breadcrumbs, paprika, salt, and black pepper.
3. Dip each cod fillet in beaten egg, then coat it with the coconut breadcrumb mixture.
4. Lightly brush olive oil on both sides of each coated fillet.
5. Place the cod fillets in the air fryer basket.
6. Air fry at 200°C for about 10-12 minutes or until the fish is cooked through and the coating is crispy and golden brown.
7. Serve the crispy coconut-crusted cod fillets hot.

## Stuffed Peppers with Quinoa and Black Beans

Serves: 4
Prep time: 20 minutes / Cook time: 20 minutes

**Ingredients:**
- 4 bell peppers, halved and seeds removed
- 150g quinoa, cooked

- 200g black beans, cooked
- 1 onion, finely chopped
- 2 cloves garlic, minced
- 1 tsp ground cumin
- 1 tsp paprika
- 100g grated cheddar cheese
- 2 tbsp chopped fresh parsley
- Salt and black pepper, to taste

**Preparation instructions:**
1. Preheat the Air Fryer to 180°C for 5 minutes.
2. In a pan, sauté onion and garlic until softened.
3. Add cooked quinoa, black beans, ground cumin, paprika, salt, and black pepper to the pan. Mix well and cook for a few more minutes.
4. Fill each bell pepper half with the quinoa and black bean mixture.
5. Sprinkle grated cheddar cheese on top of each stuffed pepper.
6. Place the stuffed peppers in the air fryer basket.
7. Air fry at 180°C for about 18-20 minutes or until the peppers are tender and the cheese is melted and bubbly.
8. Garnish with chopped fresh parsley before serving.

## Honey Mustard Glazed Air Fryer Lamb Chops

Serves: 4
Prep time: 10 minutes / Cook time: 12 minutes

**Ingredients:**
- 8 lamb loin chops
- 60ml honey
- 2 tbsp Dijon mustard
- 1 tbsp olive oil
- 2 cloves garlic, minced
- 1 tsp dried rosemary
- Salt and black pepper, to taste

**Preparation instructions:**
1. Preheat the Air Fryer to 200°C for 5 minutes.
2. In a bowl, whisk together honey, Dijon mustard, olive oil, minced garlic, dried rosemary, salt, and black pepper.
3. Coat the lamb chops with the honey mustard glaze.
4. Place the lamb chops in the air fryer basket.
5. Air fry at 200°C for about 10-12 minutes, turning halfway through, until the lamb is cooked to your desired doneness.
6. Rest the lamb chops for a few minutes before serving.

## Air Fried Veggie and Chickpea Curry

Serves: 4
Prep time: 15 minutes / Cook time: 20 minutes

**Ingredients:**
- 400g canned chickpeas, drained and rinsed
- 200g mixed vegetables (such as bell peppers, peas, carrots)
- 1 onion, finely chopped
- 2 cloves garlic, minced
- 400ml coconut milk
- 2 tbsp curry powder
- 1 tbsp olive oil
- Fresh coriander leaves (for garnish)
- Salt, to taste

**Preparation instructions:**
1. Preheat the Air Fryer to 180°C for 5 minutes.
2. In a pan, heat olive oil and sauté chopped onion and minced garlic until softened.
3. Add mixed vegetables to the pan and cook for a few minutes.
4. Stir in curry powder and salt, then pour in coconut milk.
5. Add chickpeas to the pan and let the mixture simmer for about 10 minutes.
6. Transfer the curry mixture into the air fryer basket.
7. Air fry at 180°C for about 15-20 minutes, stirring occasionally, until the vegetables are tender and the curry thickens.
8. Garnish with fresh coriander leaves before serving.

## Air Fryer Beef Stir-Fry with Mixed Vegetables

Serves: 4
Prep time: 20 minutes / Cook time: 15 minutes

**Ingredients:**
- 400g beef steak, thinly sliced
- 200g mixed vegetables (such as broccoli, bell peppers, carrots)
- 1 onion, sliced
- 2 cloves garlic, minced
- 3 tbsp soy sauce
- 2 tbsp oyster sauce
- 1 tbsp olive oil
- 1 tsp cornflour (cornstarch)
- Salt and black pepper, to taste

**Preparation instructions:**
1. Preheat the Air Fryer to 200°C for 5 minutes.

2. In a bowl, mix soy sauce, oyster sauce, cornflour, salt, and black pepper.
3. Marinate the beef slices in the prepared sauce for about 10 minutes.
4. In a pan, heat olive oil and sauté sliced onion and minced garlic until fragrant.
5. Add the marinated beef to the pan and stir-fry until browned.
6. Add mixed vegetables to the pan and continue stir-frying for a few more minutes until the vegetables are slightly tender.
7. Transfer the beef and vegetable stir-fry into the air fryer basket.
8. Air fry at 200°C for about 10-12 minutes, stirring occasionally, until the beef is cooked and the vegetables are cooked to your liking.
9. Serve the beef stir-fry hot.

## Buttermilk Fried Air Fryer Chicken

Serves: 4
Prep time: 20 minutes / Cook time: 20 minutes

**Ingredients:**
- 8 chicken drumsticks or thighs, skin-on
- 250ml buttermilk
- 100g plain flour
- 1 tsp paprika
- 1 tsp garlic powder
- 1 tsp onion powder
- 1/2 tsp cayenne pepper (optional)
- Salt and black pepper, to taste
- Cooking spray or oil, for greasing

**Preparation instructions:**
1. Preheat the Air Fryer to 200°C for 5 minutes.
2. In a bowl, mix buttermilk with salt and black pepper.
3. In another bowl, combine plain flour, paprika, garlic powder, onion powder, cayenne pepper, salt, and black pepper.
4. Dip each chicken piece into the buttermilk mixture, then dredge it in the seasoned flour mixture, coating evenly.
5. Lightly grease the air fryer basket with cooking spray or oil.
6. Place the coated chicken pieces in the basket, leaving space between each piece.
7. Air fry at 200°C for about 18-20 minutes, turning once halfway through, until the chicken is golden and cooked through.
8. Serve the buttermilk fried chicken hot.

## Sticky Maple Glazed Air Fryer Salmon

Serves: 4
Prep time: 10 minutes / Cook time: 12 minutes

**Ingredients:**
- 4 salmon fillets (about 150g each)
- 60ml maple syrup
- 2 tbsp soy sauce
- 1 tbsp olive oil
- 2 cloves garlic, minced
- 1 tsp grated ginger
- Salt and black pepper, to taste

**Preparation instructions:**
1. Preheat the Air Fryer to 200°C for 5 minutes.
2. In a bowl, whisk together maple syrup, soy sauce, olive oil, minced garlic, grated ginger, salt, and black pepper.
3. Coat the salmon fillets with the maple glaze.
4. Place the salmon fillets in the air fryer basket.
5. Air fry at 200°C for about 10-12 minutes or until the salmon is cooked through and caramelized.
6. Serve the sticky maple glazed salmon hot.

## Air Fried Veggie Frittata

Serves: 4
Prep time: 15 minutes / Cook time: 20 minutes

**Ingredients:**
- 8 large eggs
- 100ml milk
- 100g grated cheddar cheese
- 1 onion, chopped
- 1 bell pepper, chopped
- 100g mushrooms, sliced
- 2 handfuls spinach leaves
- 1 tbsp olive oil
- Salt and black pepper, to taste

**Preparation instructions:**
1. Preheat the Air Fryer to 180°C for 5 minutes.
2. In a bowl, whisk together eggs, milk, grated cheddar cheese, salt, and black pepper.
3. In a pan, heat olive oil and sauté chopped onion until translucent.
4. Add chopped bell pepper and sliced mushrooms to the pan. Cook until softened.
5. Add spinach leaves to the pan and cook until wilted.
6. Spread the cooked vegetables evenly in the air

fryer basket.
7. Pour the egg mixture over the vegetables.
8. Air fry at 180°C for about 18-20 minutes or until the frittata is set and the top is golden.
9. Allow the frittata to cool slightly before slicing and serving.

## Air Fryer Turkey Meatballs with Marinara Sauce

Serves: 4
Prep time: 15 minutes / Cook time: 20 minutes

**Ingredients:**
- 500g ground turkey
- 50g breadcrumbs
- 1 egg
- 30ml milk
- 1 clove garlic, minced
- 1 tsp dried oregano
- 1/2 tsp dried basil
- Salt and black pepper, to taste
- 500ml marinara sauce

**Preparation instructions:**
1. Preheat the Air Fryer to 180°C for 5 minutes.
2. In a bowl, combine ground turkey, breadcrumbs, egg, milk, minced garlic, dried oregano, dried basil, salt, and black pepper. Mix until well combined.
3. Shape the mixture into meatballs of even size.
4. Place the meatballs in the air fryer basket.
5. Air fry at 180°C for about 15-18 minutes or until the meatballs are cooked through.
6. In a saucepan, heat the marinara sauce.
7. Once the meatballs are cooked, transfer them to the marinara sauce and simmer for a few minutes.
8. Serve the turkey meatballs with marinara sauce.

## Mediterranean Style Air Fryer Lamb Kebabs

Serves: 4
Prep time: 20 minutes / Cook time: 15 minutes

**Ingredients:**
- 500g lamb, cubed
- 1 tbsp olive oil
- 2 cloves garlic, minced
- 1 tsp dried oregano
- 1 tsp dried thyme
- Juice of 1 lemon
- Salt and black pepper, to taste
- Skewers

**Preparation instructions:**
1. Preheat the Air Fryer to 200°C for 5 minutes.
2. In a bowl, mix cubed lamb with olive oil, minced garlic, dried oregano, dried thyme, lemon juice, salt, and black pepper. Ensure the lamb is evenly coated.
3. Thread the seasoned lamb onto skewers.
4. Place the lamb skewers in the air fryer basket.
5. Air fry at 200°C for about 12-15 minutes or until the lamb is cooked to your desired doneness.
6. Serve the Mediterranean-style lamb kebabs hot.

## Stuffed Portobello Mushrooms with Spinach and Goat Cheese

Serves: 4
Prep time: 15 minutes / Cook time: 12 minutes

**Ingredients:**
- 4 large Portobello mushrooms
- 200g fresh spinach, chopped
- 100g goat cheese
- 2 cloves garlic, minced
- 2 tbsp olive oil
- Salt and black pepper, to taste

**Preparation instructions:**
1. Preheat the Air Fryer to 180°C for 5 minutes.
2. Remove the stems from the Portobello mushrooms and clean the caps.
3. In a pan, heat olive oil and sauté minced garlic until fragrant.
4. Add chopped spinach to the pan and cook until wilted.
5. Season the spinach with salt and black pepper.
6. Stuff each Portobello mushroom cap with the sautéed spinach mixture.
7. Crumble goat cheese over the stuffed mushrooms.
8. Place the stuffed mushrooms in the air fryer basket.
9. Air fry at 180°C for about 10-12 minutes or until the mushrooms are tender and the cheese is melted.
10. Serve the stuffed Portobello mushrooms warm.

## Air Fried Honey Garlic Tofu

Serves: 4
Prep time: 20 minutes / Cook time: 15 minutes

**Ingredients:**
- 400g firm tofu, drained and cubed
- 3 tbsp soy sauce
- 2 tbsp honey
- 2 cloves garlic, minced
- 1 tbsp olive oil
- Sesame seeds, for garnish
- Chopped spring onions, for garnish

**Preparation instructions:**
1. Preheat the Air Fryer to 200°C for 5 minutes.
2. In a bowl, mix cubed tofu with soy sauce, honey, minced garlic, and olive oil. Allow it to marinate for about 10-15 minutes.
3. Place the marinated tofu cubes in the air fryer basket in a single layer.
4. Air fry at 200°C for about 12-15 minutes, shaking the basket or turning the tofu halfway through, until crispy and golden.
5. Once cooked, garnish the honey garlic tofu with sesame seeds and chopped spring onions before serving.

## Pesto and Mozzarella Stuffed Air Fryer Chicken Breasts

Serves: 4
Prep time: 15 minutes / Cook time: 20 minutes

**Ingredients:**
- 4 boneless, skinless chicken breasts
- 4 tbsp pesto sauce
- 100g mozzarella cheese, sliced
- Salt and black pepper, to taste
- Olive oil, for brushing

**Preparation instructions:**
1. Preheat the Air Fryer to 180°C for 5 minutes.
2. Cut a pocket into each chicken breast without cutting all the way through.
3. Season the chicken breasts with salt and black pepper.
4. Spoon 1 tablespoon of pesto sauce into each pocket of the chicken breasts.
5. Stuff each chicken breast with mozzarella cheese slices.
6. Secure the openings with toothpicks if needed.
7. Lightly brush the chicken breasts with olive oil.
8. Place the chicken breasts in the air fryer basket.
9. Air fry at 180°C for about 18-20 minutes or until the chicken is cooked through and the cheese is melted and bubbly.
10. Let the chicken breasts rest for a few minutes before serving.

## BBQ Pulled Pork Sliders

Serves: 4
Prep time: 15 minutes / Cook time: 25 minutes

**Ingredients:**
- 500g pork shoulder, cooked and shredded
- 120ml barbecue sauce
- 8 slider buns
- Coleslaw, for serving (optional)

**Preparation instructions:**
1. Preheat the Air Fryer to 180°C for 5 minutes.
2. In a bowl, mix shredded pork shoulder with barbecue sauce until well combined.
3. Place the BBQ pork mixture in the air fryer basket.
4. Air fry at 180°C for about 20-25 minutes or until the pork is heated through and slightly caramelized.
5. Toast the slider buns in the air fryer for a minute, if desired.
6. Assemble the slider buns with BBQ pulled pork and coleslaw, if using.
7. Serve the BBQ pulled pork sliders warm.

## Crispy Garlic Parmesan Air Fryer Brussels Sprouts

Serves: 4
Prep time: 10 minutes / Cook time: 15 minutes

**Ingredients:**
- 500g Brussels sprouts, trimmed and halved
- 2 tbsp olive oil
- 2 cloves garlic, minced
- 50g grated Parmesan cheese
- Salt and black pepper, to taste

**Preparation instructions:**
1. Preheat the Air Fryer to 200°C for 5 minutes.
2. In a bowl, toss Brussels sprouts with olive oil, minced garlic, salt, and black pepper until coated.
3. Place the Brussels sprouts in the air fryer basket.
4. Air fry at 200°C for about 12-15 minutes, shaking the basket halfway through, until crispy and golden.
5. Sprinkle grated Parmesan cheese over the Brussels sprouts and toss to combine.
6. Air fry for an additional minute until the cheese melts and turns golden.
7. Serve the crispy garlic Parmesan Brussels sprouts hot.

## Jamaican Jerk Chicken Wings

Serves: 4
Prep time: 15 minutes / Cook time: 25 minutes

**Ingredients:**
- 1kg chicken wings, separated into drumettes and flats
- 3 tbsp Jamaican jerk seasoning
- 2 tbsp olive oil
- 1 lime, juiced
- Salt, to taste

**Preparation instructions:**
1. Preheat the Air Fryer to 200°C for 5 minutes.
2. In a bowl, toss chicken wings with Jamaican jerk seasoning, olive oil, lime juice, and salt until evenly coated.
3. Place the seasoned chicken wings in the air fryer basket in a single layer.
4. Air fry at 200°C for about 20-25 minutes, flipping the wings halfway through, until they are crispy and cooked through.
5. Serve the Jamaican jerk chicken wings hot.

## Air Fryer Beef and Broccoli

Serves: 4
Prep time: 15 minutes / Cook time: 15 minutes

**Ingredients:**
- 500g beef sirloin or flank steak, thinly sliced
- 200g broccoli florets
- 3 tbsp soy sauce
- 2 tbsp oyster sauce
- 1 tbsp brown sugar
- 2 cloves garlic, minced
- 1 tsp grated ginger
- 1 tsp cornflour (cornstarch)
- 2 tbsp water
- 1 tbsp sesame oil
- 1 tbsp olive oil
- Sesame seeds, for garnish
- Cooked rice, for serving

**Preparation instructions:**
1. Preheat the Air Fryer to 200°C for 5 minutes.
2. In a bowl, mix soy sauce, oyster sauce, brown sugar, minced garlic, grated ginger, cornflour, water, and sesame oil to make the sauce. Set aside.
3. In a pan or wok, heat olive oil and stir-fry beef slices until browned. Remove and set aside.
4. Add broccoli florets to the pan and stir-fry for a few minutes until slightly tender.
5. Return the cooked beef to the pan with the broccoli.
6. Pour the prepared sauce over the beef and broccoli, stirring to coat evenly.
7. Transfer the beef and broccoli mixture to the air fryer basket.
8. Air fry at 200°C for about 8-10 minutes or until the sauce thickens and coats the beef and broccoli.
9. Sprinkle sesame seeds over the beef and broccoli.
10. Serve the beef and broccoli over cooked rice.

## Cheesy Cauliflower Bake

Serves: 4
Prep time: 15 minutes / Cook time: 25 minutes

**Ingredients:**
- 1 large cauliflower, cut into florets
- 200ml double cream
- 100g grated cheddar cheese
- 50g grated Parmesan cheese
- 2 cloves garlic, minced
- 1 tsp dried thyme
- Salt and black pepper, to taste
- 50g breadcrumbs
- 2 tbsp chopped parsley, for garnish

**Preparation instructions:**
1. Preheat the Air Fryer to 180°C for 5 minutes.
2. Steam or boil cauliflower florets until just tender. Drain well.
3. In a saucepan, heat double cream, grated cheddar cheese, grated Parmesan cheese, minced garlic, dried thyme, salt, and black pepper. Stir until the cheeses melt and the sauce thickens slightly.
4. Add the cooked cauliflower to the cheese sauce and toss to coat evenly.
5. Transfer the cauliflower and cheese mixture to an oven-proof dish.
6. Sprinkle breadcrumbs over the top of the cauliflower mixture.
7. Place the dish in the air fryer basket.
8. Air fry at 180°C for about 20-25 minutes or until the top is golden and bubbly.
9. Garnish with chopped parsley before serving.

## Air Fryer Sticky Orange Ginger Glazed Duck Breast

Serves: 4

Prep time: 15 minutes / Cook time: 20 minutes

**Ingredients:**
- 4 duck breasts
- 80ml orange juice
- Zest of 1 orange
- 2 tbsp honey
- 2 tbsp soy sauce
- 1 tbsp grated ginger
- 2 cloves garlic, minced
- Salt and black pepper, to taste

**Preparation instructions:**
1. Preheat the Air Fryer to 180°C for 5 minutes.
2. In a bowl, mix orange juice, orange zest, honey, soy sauce, grated ginger, minced garlic, salt, and black pepper to create the glaze.
3. Score the skin of the duck breasts and season with salt and black pepper.
4. Brush the duck breasts with the glaze on both sides.
5. Place the duck breasts in the air fryer basket.
6. Air fry at 180°C for about 15-18 minutes, glazing occasionally, until the duck is cooked to your desired doneness.
7. Rest the duck breasts for a few minutes before slicing and serving.

## Stuffed Zucchini Boats with Ground Turkey and Cheese

Serves: 4
Prep time: 20 minutes / Cook time: 18 minutes

**Ingredients:**
- 4 medium zucchinis
- 300g ground turkey
- 100g shredded cheddar cheese
- 1 small onion, diced
- 2 cloves garlic, minced
- 1 tsp dried oregano
- 1 tsp dried basil
- Salt and black pepper, to taste
- Olive oil

**Preparation instructions:**
1. Preheat the Air Fryer to 180°C for 5 minutes.
2. Cut the zucchinis in half lengthwise and scoop out the flesh to create boats.
3. In a pan, heat olive oil and sauté diced onion and minced garlic until softened.
4. Add ground turkey to the pan and cook until browned.
5. Season the turkey with dried oregano, dried basil, salt, and black pepper.
6. Fill each zucchini boat with the cooked turkey mixture.
7. Sprinkle shredded cheddar cheese over the stuffed zucchinis.
8. Place the stuffed zucchini boats in the air fryer basket.
9. Air fry at 180°C for about 15-18 minutes or until the zucchinis are tender and the cheese is melted and bubbly.
10. Serve the stuffed zucchini boats hot.

## Crispy Coconut-Curry Air Fryer Prawns

Serves: 4
Prep time: 15 minutes / Cook time: 10 minutes

**Ingredients:**
- 500g large prawns, peeled and deveined
- 50g breadcrumbs
- 50g shredded coconut
- 2 tbsp curry powder
- 1 egg, beaten
- Salt and black pepper, to taste
- Cooking spray

**Preparation instructions:**
1. Preheat the Air Fryer to 200°C for 5 minutes.
2. In a bowl, mix breadcrumbs, shredded coconut, curry powder, salt, and black pepper.
3. Dip each prawn in beaten egg, then coat with the breadcrumb mixture.
4. Lightly spray the air fryer basket with cooking spray.
5. Place the coated prawns in the air fryer basket in a single layer.
6. Air fry at 200°C for about 8-10 minutes or until the prawns are crispy and cooked through.
7. Serve the crispy coconut-curry prawns with your favourite dipping sauce.

## Air Fried Balsamic Glazed Veggie Skewers

Serves: 4
Prep time: 15 minutes / Cook time: 12 minutes

**Ingredients:**
- 2 courgettes, sliced
- 2 bell peppers, diced

- 1 red onion, cut into chunks
- 200g cherry tomatoes
- 60ml balsamic vinegar
- 2 tbsp olive oil
- 2 cloves garlic, minced
- 1 tsp dried mixed herbs
- Salt and black pepper, to taste
- Wooden skewers, soaked in water

**Preparation instructions:**
1. Preheat the Air Fryer to 200°C for 5 minutes.
2. Thread the sliced courgettes, diced bell peppers, red onion chunks, and cherry tomatoes onto the soaked wooden skewers.
3. In a bowl, whisk together balsamic vinegar, olive oil, minced garlic, dried mixed herbs, salt, and black pepper to make the glaze.
4. Brush the vegetable skewers with the balsamic glaze on all sides.
5. Place the vegetable skewers in the air fryer basket.
6. Air fry at 200°C for about 10-12 minutes, turning the skewers halfway through, until the vegetables are tender and slightly charred.
7. Serve the balsamic glazed veggie skewers hot.

## Garlic Parmesan Crusted Air Fryer Lamb Chops

Serves: 4
Prep time: 15 minutes / Cook time: 12 minutes

**Ingredients:**
- 8 lamb loin chops
- 50g grated Parmesan cheese
- 2 cloves garlic, minced
- 2 tbsp fresh parsley, chopped
- 2 tbsp olive oil
- Salt and black pepper, to taste

**Preparation instructions:**
1. Preheat the Air Fryer to 200°C for 5 minutes.
2. In a bowl, mix grated Parmesan cheese, minced garlic, chopped fresh parsley, salt, and black pepper.
3. Brush each lamb chop with olive oil on both sides.
4. Press the Parmesan mixture onto both sides of each lamb chop to create a crust.
5. Place the lamb chops in the air fryer basket.
6. Air fry at 200°C for about 10-12 minutes or until the lamb chops are cooked to your desired doneness and the crust is golden and crispy.
7. Allow the lamb chops to rest for a few minutes before serving.

## Tex-Mex Air Fryer Stuffed Peppers

Serves: 4
Prep time: 20 minutes / Cook time: 15 minutes

**Ingredients:**
- 4 bell peppers, halved and deseeded
- 300g cooked rice
- 200g black beans, drained and rinsed
- 200g sweetcorn kernels
- 1 red onion, diced
- 1 tsp ground cumin
- 1 tsp smoked paprika
- 1/2 tsp chilli powder
- 100g shredded cheddar cheese
- Fresh coriander, chopped, for garnish
- Cooking spray

**Preparation instructions:**
1. Preheat the Air Fryer to 180°C for 5 minutes.
2. In a bowl, mix cooked rice, black beans, sweetcorn kernels, diced red onion, ground cumin, smoked paprika, and chilli powder.
3. Stuff each bell pepper half with the rice and bean mixture.
4. Sprinkle shredded cheddar cheese over the stuffed peppers.
5. Lightly spray the air fryer basket with cooking spray.
6. Place the stuffed peppers in the air fryer basket.
7. Air fry at 180°C for about 12-15 minutes or until the peppers are tender and the cheese is melted and bubbly.
8. Garnish the Tex-Mex stuffed peppers with chopped fresh coriander before serving.

## Lemon-Herb Butter Air Fryer Lobster Tails

Serves: 4
Prep time: 15 minutes / Cook time: 10 minutes

**Ingredients:**
- 4 lobster tails, split in half lengthwise
- 50g unsalted butter, melted
- Zest of 1 lemon
- 2 tbsp chopped fresh parsley
- 2 cloves garlic, minced
- Salt and black pepper, to taste
- Lemon wedges, for serving

**Preparation instructions:**
1. Preheat the Air Fryer to 200°C for 5 minutes.

2. In a bowl, mix melted unsalted butter, lemon zest, chopped fresh parsley, minced garlic, salt, and black pepper to make the herb butter.
3. Brush the lobster tails with the herb butter on the flesh side.
4. Place the lobster tails in the air fryer basket, flesh side up.
5. Air fry at 200°C for about 8-10 minutes or until the lobster meat is opaque and cooked through.
6. Serve the lemon-herb butter lobster tails with lemon wedges.

## Air Fried Chicken Cordon Bleu

Serves: 4

Prep time: 20 minutes / Cook time: 20 minutes

**Ingredients:**
- 4 chicken breasts, pounded thin
- 4 slices ham
- 4 slices Swiss cheese
- 100g breadcrumbs
- 50g grated Parmesan cheese
- 2 eggs, beaten
- 2 tbsp olive oil
- Salt and black pepper, to taste
- Toothpicks

**Preparation instructions:**
1. Preheat the Air Fryer to 180°C for 5 minutes.
2. Season chicken breasts with salt and black pepper.
3. Place a slice of ham and a slice of Swiss cheese on each chicken breast.
4. Roll up each chicken breast, securing with toothpicks to hold the filling.
5. In a bowl, mix breadcrumbs and grated Parmesan cheese.
6. Dip each chicken roll in beaten egg, then coat with the breadcrumb mixture.
7. Lightly brush or spray olive oil on the coated chicken rolls.
8. Place the chicken rolls in the air fryer basket.
9. Air fry at 180°C for about 18-20 minutes or until the chicken is cooked through and the coating is golden and crispy.
10. Remove toothpicks before serving.

## Crispy Breaded Air Fryer Pork Schnitzel

Serves: 4

Prep time: 20 minutes / Cook time: 15 minutes

**Ingredients:**
- 4 pork loin steaks, pounded thin
- 100g plain flour
- 2 eggs, beaten
- 150g breadcrumbs
- 50g grated Parmesan cheese
- 2 tsp paprika
- 2 tsp dried thyme
- Salt and black pepper, to taste
- Cooking spray
- Lemon wedges, for serving

**Preparation instructions:**
1. Preheat the Air Fryer to 200°C for 5 minutes.
2. Season pork loin steaks with salt and black pepper.
3. Set up three shallow bowls: one with flour, one with beaten eggs, and one with a mixture of breadcrumbs, grated Parmesan cheese, paprika, dried thyme, salt, and black pepper.
4. Dredge each pork steak in flour, then dip in beaten egg, and coat with the breadcrumb mixture.
5. Lightly spray the air fryer basket with cooking spray.
6. Place the breaded pork steaks in the air fryer basket.
7. Air fry at 200°C for about 12-15 minutes, flipping halfway through, until the pork is golden and cooked through.
8. Serve the crispy breaded pork schnitzel with lemon wedges.

## Vegan Air Fryer Tofu Tikka Masala

Serves: 4

Prep time: 20 minutes / Cook time: 20 minutes

**Ingredients:**
- 400g firm tofu, pressed and cubed
- 2 tbsp vegetable oil
- 1 onion, finely chopped
- 2 cloves garlic, minced
- 1 tsp grated ginger
- 1 tsp ground cumin
- 1 tsp ground coriander
- 1/2 tsp ground turmeric
- 1/2 tsp garam masala
- 1/4 tsp cayenne pepper (adjust to taste)
- 200g tomato passata
- 150ml coconut milk
- 2 tbsp chopped fresh coriander

- Salt and black pepper, to taste

**Preparation instructions:**
1. Preheat the Air Fryer to 180°C for 5 minutes.
2. In a bowl, toss tofu cubes with 1 tablespoon of vegetable oil and a pinch of salt.
3. Place the tofu cubes in the air fryer basket.
4. Air fry at 180°C for about 12-15 minutes, shaking the basket occasionally, until the tofu is crispy and golden. Set aside.
5. In a pan, heat 1 tablespoon of vegetable oil and sauté finely chopped onion until translucent.
6. Add minced garlic and grated ginger to the pan, and cook for another minute.
7. Stir in ground cumin, ground coriander, ground turmeric, garam masala, cayenne pepper, and cook for a minute until fragrant.
8. Pour in tomato passata and coconut milk, stirring to combine.
9. Add the air-fried tofu cubes to the sauce and simmer for 5-7 minutes until the sauce thickens.
10. Season with salt and black pepper to taste.
11. Garnish with chopped fresh coriander before serving the vegan tofu tikka masala.

## Air Fryer Teriyaki Glazed Beef Skewers

Serves: 4
Prep time: 15 minutes / Cook time: 12 minutes

**Ingredients:**
- 500g beef sirloin, cubed
- 80ml soy sauce
- 60ml mirin
- 2 tbsp honey
- 1 tbsp rice vinegar
- 2 cloves garlic, minced
- 1 tsp grated ginger
- Sesame seeds and chopped spring onions for garnish

**Preparation instructions:**
1. Preheat the Air Fryer to 200°C for 5 minutes.
2. In a bowl, mix soy sauce, mirin, honey, rice vinegar, minced garlic, and grated ginger to create the teriyaki marinade.
3. Thread the beef cubes onto skewers and place them in a shallow dish. Pour the marinade over the beef skewers and let them marinate for 10 minutes.
4. Place the beef skewers in the air fryer basket.
5. Air fry at 200°C for 10-12 minutes, turning once, until the beef is cooked to your liking and slightly charred.
6. Garnish with sesame seeds and chopped spring onions before serving.

## Moroccan Spiced Air Fryer Chickpea Stew

Serves: 4
Prep time: 15 minutes / Cook time: 20 minutes

**Ingredients:**
- 400g canned chickpeas, drained and rinsed
- 400g canned chopped tomatoes
- 1 onion, finely chopped
- 2 cloves garlic, minced
- 1 red bell pepper, diced
- 1 carrot, diced
- 1 tsp ground cumin
- 1 tsp ground coriander
- 1/2 tsp smoked paprika
- 1/4 tsp ground cinnamon
- 250ml vegetable stock
- Fresh coriander leaves, for garnish
- Cooked couscous or rice, for serving

**Preparation instructions:**
1. Preheat the Air Fryer to 180°C for 5 minutes.
2. In a bowl, mix chickpeas, chopped tomatoes, onion, minced garlic, diced red bell pepper, diced carrot, ground cumin, ground coriander, smoked paprika, and ground cinnamon.
3. Pour the mixture into the air fryer basket and spread it evenly.
4. Air fry at 180°C for 18-20 minutes, stirring halfway through, until the vegetables are tender and the stew thickens.
5. Serve the Moroccan spiced chickpea stew over cooked couscous or rice.
6. Garnish with fresh coriander leaves.

## Air Fried Stuffed Portobello Mushroom Caps with Sun-Dried Tomatoes

Serves: 4
Prep time: 15 minutes / Cook time: 12 minutes

**Ingredients:**
- 4 large Portobello mushroom caps
- 100g cream cheese
- 50g sun-dried tomatoes, chopped
- 2 tbsp grated Parmesan cheese
- 2 tbsp chopped fresh parsley

- 1 clove garlic, minced
- Salt and black pepper, to taste
- Olive oil for drizzling

**Preparation instructions:**
1. Preheat the Air Fryer to 180°C for 5 minutes.
2. In a bowl, mix cream cheese, sun-dried tomatoes, grated Parmesan cheese, chopped fresh parsley, minced garlic, salt, and black pepper to create the stuffing.
3. Remove the stems from the Portobello mushroom caps and gently scrape out the gills.
4. Fill each mushroom cap with the prepared stuffing mixture.
5. Drizzle a little olive oil over the stuffed mushroom caps.
6. Place the stuffed mushroom caps in the air fryer basket.
7. Air fry at 180°C for 10-12 minutes or until the mushrooms are cooked, and the filling is hot and slightly browned.
8. Serve the air-fried stuffed Portobello mushroom caps as a delicious appetizer or side dish.

## BBQ Pulled Jackfruit Sandwiches

Serves: 4
Prep time: 15 minutes / Cook time: 15 minutes

**Ingredients:**
- 2 cans (400g each) young green jackfruit in brine, drained and shredded
- 250ml BBQ sauce
- 1 onion, finely chopped
- 2 cloves garlic, minced
- 1 tbsp olive oil
- 4 burger buns
- Coleslaw (optional), for serving

**Preparation instructions:**
1. Preheat the Air Fryer to 180°C for 5 minutes.
2. In a pan, heat olive oil and sauté finely chopped onion and minced garlic until softened.
3. Add shredded jackfruit to the pan and cook for a few minutes.
4. Pour BBQ sauce over the jackfruit, stirring to coat evenly.
5. Transfer the BBQ jackfruit mixture to the air fryer basket.
6. Air fry at 180°C for 12-15 minutes, stirring occasionally, until the jackfruit is hot and slightly caramelized.
7. Toast the burger buns if desired.
8. Spoon the BBQ pulled jackfruit onto the bottom half of each bun.
9. Top with coleslaw if preferred and cover with the top half of the bun.
10. Serve the BBQ pulled jackfruit sandwiches.

## Air Fryer Honey Mustard Glazed Turkey Breast

Serves: 4
Prep time: 10 minutes / Cook time: 30 minutes

**Ingredients:**
- 600g turkey breast fillet
- 60ml honey
- 2 tbsp Dijon mustard
- 1 tbsp wholegrain mustard
- 1 tbsp olive oil
- 1 clove garlic, minced
- Salt and black pepper, to taste
- Fresh thyme leaves, for garnish

**Preparation instructions:**
1. Preheat the Air Fryer to 180°C for 5 minutes.
2. In a bowl, whisk together honey, Dijon mustard, wholegrain mustard, olive oil, minced garlic, salt, and black pepper to create the glaze.
3. Season the turkey breast fillet with salt and black pepper.
4. Brush the turkey breast with the prepared honey mustard glaze.
5. Place the turkey breast in the air fryer basket.
6. Air fry at 180°C for 25-30 minutes or until the turkey is cooked through, brushing with more glaze halfway through cooking.
7. Let the turkey breast rest for a few minutes before slicing.
8. Garnish with fresh thyme leaves before serving.

## Herbed Air Fried Rack of Lamb

Serves: 4
Prep time: 10 minutes / Cook time: 25 minutes

**Ingredients:**
- 2 racks of lamb (about 500g each), trimmed and frenched
- 2 tbsp olive oil
- 2 cloves garlic, minced
- 2 tsp chopped fresh rosemary
- 2 tsp chopped fresh thyme

- Salt and black pepper, to taste
- Lemon wedges, for serving

**Preparation instructions:**
1. Preheat the Air Fryer to 200°C for 5 minutes.
2. In a bowl, mix olive oil, minced garlic, chopped fresh rosemary, chopped fresh thyme, salt, and black pepper.
3. Rub the herb mixture all over the racks of lamb.
4. Place the racks of lamb in the air fryer basket, bone side down.
5. Air fry at 200°C for 20-25 minutes for medium-rare, adjusting time for desired doneness, flipping the racks halfway through.
6. Let the lamb rest for a few minutes before slicing into chops.
7. Serve the herbed air-fried rack of lamb with lemon wedges.

## Crispy Air Fryer Polenta Fries

Serves: 4
Prep time: 10 minutes / Cook time: 20 minutes

**Ingredients:**
- 250g instant polenta
- 1 litre vegetable stock
- 50g grated Parmesan cheese
- 1 tsp garlic powder
- 1 tsp dried oregano
- 1 tsp paprika
- Cooking spray
- Salt and black pepper, to taste

**Preparation instructions:**
1. In a saucepan, bring vegetable stock to a boil.
2. Gradually whisk in instant polenta and cook according to package instructions until thickened.
3. Remove from heat and stir in grated Parmesan cheese, garlic powder, dried oregano, paprika, salt, and black pepper.
4. Pour the polenta into a square baking dish lined with parchment paper, spreading it evenly.
5. Refrigerate for 1-2 hours until set.
6. Preheat the Air Fryer to 200°C for 5 minutes.
7. Remove the set polenta from the baking dish and cut it into fries.
8. Lightly spray the air fryer basket with cooking spray.
9. Place the polenta fries in the air fryer basket in a single layer.
10. Air fry at 200°C for 18-20 minutes or until the polenta fries are crispy and golden brown.
11. Season with additional salt and black pepper if needed before serving.

## Jamaican Jerk Air Fryer Pork Tenderloin

Serves: 4
Prep time: 15 minutes / Cook time: 25 minutes

**Ingredients:**
- 600g pork tenderloin
- 2 tbsp Jamaican jerk seasoning
- 2 tbsp olive oil
- 2 tbsp lime juice
- 1 tsp brown sugar
- Salt, to taste
- Fresh coriander leaves, for garnish

**Preparation instructions:**
1. Preheat the Air Fryer to 180°C for 5 minutes.
2. In a bowl, mix Jamaican jerk seasoning, olive oil, lime juice, brown sugar, and salt to create the marinade.
3. Coat the pork tenderloin with the prepared marinade.
4. Place the pork tenderloin in the air fryer basket.
5. Air fry at 180°C for 22-25 minutes, flipping once halfway through cooking, until the pork is cooked through and reaches an internal temperature of 63°C.
6. Let the pork tenderloin rest for a few minutes before slicing.
7. Garnish with fresh coriander leaves before serving.

## Mediterranean Style Air Fryer Veggie Platter with Tzatziki

Serves: 4
Prep time: 15 minutes / Cook time: 12 minutes

**Ingredients:**
- 400g mixed Mediterranean vegetables (zucchini, bell peppers, cherry tomatoes)
- 2 tbsp olive oil
- 1 tsp dried oregano
- 1 tsp paprika
- Salt and black pepper, to taste
- For Tzatziki:
- 150g Greek yoghurt
- 1/2 cucumber, grated and excess liquid squeezed out
- 1 clove garlic, minced

- 1 tbsp fresh lemon juice
- 1 tbsp chopped fresh dill
- Salt and black pepper, to taste

**Preparation instructions:**
1. Preheat the Air Fryer to 200°C for 5 minutes.
2. In a bowl, toss the Mediterranean vegetables with olive oil, dried oregano, paprika, salt, and black pepper until coated.
3. Spread the seasoned vegetables in the air fryer basket in a single layer.
4. Air fry at 200°C for 12 minutes or until the vegetables are tender and slightly charred, shaking the basket halfway through the cooking time.
5. Meanwhile, prepare the Tzatziki by combining Greek yoghurt, grated cucumber, minced garlic, lemon juice, chopped dill, salt, and black pepper in a bowl. Mix well and refrigerate until serving.
6. Once the vegetables are done, serve them hot with a side of the prepared Tzatziki.

## Sticky Maple Glazed Air Fryer Duck Legs

Serves: 2
Prep time: 10 minutes / Cook time: 25 minutes

**Ingredients:**
- 2 duck legs
- 2 tbsp maple syrup
- 1 tbsp soy sauce
- 1 tbsp rice vinegar
- 1 tsp grated fresh ginger
- 1 garlic clove, minced
- 1/2 tsp Chinese five-spice powder
- Salt and black pepper, to taste
- Chopped spring onions, for garnish (optional)
- Sesame seeds, for garnish (optional)

**Preparation instructions:**
1. Preheat the Air Fryer to 180°C for 5 minutes.
2. In a bowl, combine maple syrup, soy sauce, rice vinegar, grated ginger, minced garlic, Chinese five-spice powder, salt, and black pepper.
3. Pat dry the duck legs and score the skin in a criss-cross pattern, being careful not to cut into the meat.
4. Brush the maple glaze mixture over the duck legs, ensuring they're evenly coated.
5. Place the duck legs in the air fryer basket, skin side down.
6. Air fry at 180°C for 15 minutes, then flip the duck legs, brush with more glaze, and air fry for another 10 minutes or until the skin is crispy and the duck is cooked through.
7. Once done, let the duck legs rest for a few minutes before serving. Optionally, garnish with chopped spring onions and sesame seeds before serving.

## Air Fryer Lemon Pepper Chicken Breasts

Serves: 4 people
Prep time: 10 minutes / Cooking Time: 15-18 minutes

**Ingredients:**
- 4 boneless, skinless chicken breasts (about 450 g)
- 1/2 tsp freshly ground black pepper
- 1 tsp salt
- 1 tsp dried thyme
- 2 tbsp olive oil
- 2 tbsp lemon juice
- 1 tbsp lemon zest
- 1 tsp garlic powder
- 1 cup Panko breadcrumbs

**Preparation instructions:**
1. Preheat air fryer to 200°C.
2. In a small bowl, mix together lemon zest, garlic powder, olive oil, lemon juice, salt, thyme, and black pepper.
3. Place the chicken breasts in a large bowl and cover with the lemon pepper marinade, ensuring each breast is coated well. Let the chicken marinate for 10 minutes.
4. In a shallow dish, mix together Panko breadcrumbs and remaining pepper.
5. Dip each marinated chicken breast into the breadcrumb mixture, making sure it's evenly coated.
6. Place the chicken breasts in the air fryer basket, not touching each other.
7. Cook for 15-18 minutes or until the internal temperature reaches 73.9°C.
8. Serve the lemon pepper chicken with your favourite sides. Enjoy!

## Air Fryer Whole Roasted Chicken

Serves: 4 people
Prep time: 20 minutes / Cooking Time: 30 minutes

**Ingredients:**
- 1 whole chicken, about 1.2 kg
- 4 tbsp olive oil
- 2 tsp salt
- 1 tsp black pepper
- 1 tsp dried thyme
- 1 tsp dried rosemary

**Preparation instructions:**
1. Remove the giblets and neck from inside the chicken and rinse the chicken inside and out with cold water. Pat dry with paper towels.
2. In a small bowl, mix together the olive oil, salt, pepper, thyme, and rosemary to create a marinade.
3. Rub the marinade all over the chicken, making sure to get it into all the crevices. Place the chicken in the refrigerator for 30 minutes to 1 hour to allow the flavours to penetrate.
4. Preheat your air fryer to 200°C.
5. Place the chicken in the air fryer basket and cook for 30 minutes.
6. After 30 minutes, use a meat thermometer to check the internal temperature of the chicken. The temperature should reach 74°C in the thickest part of the chicken.
7. Once the chicken is fully cooked, remove it from the air fryer and let it rest for 5-10 minutes before carving and serving.
8. Enjoy your perfectly roasted whole chicken in the air fryer!

## Chicken and Wild Mushroom Pie

Serves: 4-6 servings
Prep time: 20 minutes / Cook time: 50 minutes

**Ingredients:**
- 500 g boneless, skinless chicken breasts, cut into bite-sized pieces
- 200 g wild mushrooms (such as porcini, chanterelle, or shiitake), sliced
- 1 onion, diced
- 2 cloves garlic, minced
- 2 tablespoons butter
- 2 tablespoons all-purpose flour
- 250 ml chicken broth
- 120 ml heavy cream
- 1 teaspoon dried thyme
- Salt and pepper to taste
- 1 sheet puff pastry, thawed if frozen
- 1 egg, beaten (for egg wash)

**Preparation instructions:**
1. Preheat the oven to 200°C.
2. In a large skillet, melt the butter over medium heat. Add the diced onion and minced garlic, and sauté until the onion is translucent and fragrant.
3. Add the chicken pieces to the skillet and cook until they are browned on all sides.
4. Add the sliced wild mushrooms to the skillet and cook for another 5 minutes, until the mushrooms are softened.
5. Sprinkle the flour over the chicken and mushrooms, stirring well to coat everything evenly.
6. Slowly pour in the chicken broth and heavy cream, stirring constantly to prevent lumps from forming. Bring the mixture to a simmer and cook for a few minutes until the sauce thickens.
7. Stir in the dried thyme, and season with salt and pepper to taste. Remove the skillet from the heat.
8. Transfer the chicken and mushroom mixture to a deep pie dish or individual ramekins.
9. Roll out the puff pastry sheet on a lightly floured surface to fit the top of the pie dish or ramekins. Place the pastry over the filling, pressing the edges to seal.
10. Brush the pastry with beaten egg to create a golden and glossy finish.
11. Cut a few small slits on the top of the pastry to allow steam to escape.
12. Place the pie dish or ramekins on a baking sheet and bake in the preheated oven for about 30 minutes, or until the pastry is puffed up and golden brown.
13. Remove from the oven and let the pie cool for a few minutes before serving.
14. Serve the chicken and wild mushroom pie hot, and enjoy the delicious combination of flavours and textures.

## BBQ Glazed Air Fryer Ribs

Serves 2
Prep time: 15 minutes / Cook time: 30 minutes

**Ingredients:**
- 1 rack of baby back ribs
- 1 teaspoon salt
- 1/2 teaspoon black pepper
- 1 teaspoon garlic powder
- 1 teaspoon smoked paprika
- 1/2 cup barbecue sauce

**Preparation instructions:**
1. Begin with removing the membrane from the back of the ribs by sliding a knife under the membrane and pulling it off.
2. Combine the salt, black pepper, garlic powder, and smoked paprika in a small bowl.
3. Sprinkle the spice mixture evenly over the ribs' two sides and gently press it into place.
4. Put the curved side of the ribs up in the air fryer basket.
5. For five minutes, preheat the air fryer to 200°C.
6. Let the ribs cook in the air fryer for 25 mins at the same 200°C.
7. After 25 minutes, take the ribs out of the air fryer and slather them thoroughly in barbecue sauce.
8. Place the ribs back in the air fryer and cook for an additional five minutes.
9. Serve hot.

## Italian Seasoned Air Fryer Meatballs

Serves 4
Prep time: 15 minutes / Cook time: 15 minutes

**Ingredients:**
- 1/4 cup breadcrumbs
- 1/4 cup grated Parmesan cheese
- 1/4 cup chopped fresh parsley
- 1/2 teaspoon dried oregano
- 1/2 teaspoon dried basil
- 1/2 teaspoon garlic powder
- 1/2 teaspoon salt
- 1/4 teaspoon black pepper
- 1 egg, beaten

**Preparation instructions:**
1. Preheat the air fryer to 200°C for 5 minutes.
2. In a mixing bowl, combine the ground beef, breadcrumbs, grated Parmesan cheese, chopped fresh parsley, dried oregano, dried basil, garlic powder, salt, black pepper, and beaten egg.
3. Mix the Ingredients: until well combined, but avoid overmixing.
4. Shape the mixture into meatballs, approximately 1 inch in diameter.
5. Place the meatballs in the air fryer basket, without overcrowding them.
6. Cook the meatballs in the air fryer at 200°C for 12-15 minutes, shaking the basket gently halfway through the cooking time.
7. As soon as it's well cooked, remove the meatballs from the air fryer and let them rest for a couple of minutes before serving.

## Lamb Tagine

Serves: 4
Prep time: 20 minutes / Cook time: 2 hours

**Ingredients:**
- 800g lamb shoulder, cut into chunks
- 2 tablespoons olive oil
- 1 onion, finely chopped
- 3 cloves garlic, minced
- 2 carrots, peeled and sliced
- 2 tomatoes, diced
- 1 tablespoon tomato paste
- 1 teaspoon ground cumin
- 1 teaspoon ground coriander
- 1 teaspoon ground cinnamon
- 1/2 teaspoon ground turmeric
- 1/2 teaspoon paprika
- Salt and pepper to taste
- 500ml lamb or vegetable broth
- 1 preserved lemon, sliced (optional)
- Fresh cilantro, chopped (for garnish)

**Preparation instructions:**
1. Heat the olive oil in a large pot or tagine over medium heat. Add the chopped onion and minced garlic, and sauté until they become soft and translucent.
2. Add the lamb shoulder chunks to the pot and brown them on all sides.
3. Stir in the sliced carrots, diced tomatoes, tomato paste, ground cumin, ground coriander, ground cinnamon, ground turmeric, paprika, salt, and pepper. Mix well to coat the lamb and vegetables with the spices.
4. Pour in the lamb or vegetable broth to the pot. If using the preserved lemon, add the slices to the pot as well.
5. Cover the pot or tagine and let it simmer on low heat for about 1.5 to 2 hours, or until the lamb is tender and the flavours have melded together.
6. Taste and adjust the seasoning if needed.
7. Garnish with freshly chopped cilantro before serving.
8. Serve the Lamb Tagine hot with couscous or bread.

# Chapter 4: Beef, Pork, And Lamb

## Air Fryer Rosemary Garlic Lamb Chops

Serves: 2
Prep time: 10 minutes / Cook time: 12 minutes

**Ingredients:**
- 4 lamb chops (approximately 400g)
- 2 tbsp olive oil
- 2 cloves garlic, minced
- 1 tbsp fresh rosemary, chopped
- Salt and black pepper, to taste
- Lemon wedges, for serving (optional)

**Preparation instructions:**
1. Preheat the Air Fryer to 200°C for 5 minutes.
2. In a bowl, combine olive oil, minced garlic, chopped rosemary, salt, and black pepper.
3. Pat dry the lamb chops and coat them evenly with the prepared garlic-rosemary mixture.
4. Place the lamb chops in the air fryer basket.
5. Air fry at 200°C for 12 minutes, flipping halfway through the cooking time, until the lamb chops reach your desired level of doneness.
6. Once done, let the lamb chops rest for a couple of minutes before serving with optional lemon wedges.

## Beef and Guinness Pie Pockets

Serves: 4
Prep time: 20 minutes / Cook time: 15 minutes

**Ingredients:**
- 300g puff pastry, rolled and cut into squares
- 250g beef stew meat, cooked and shredded
- 100ml Guinness beer
- 1 onion, finely chopped
- 2 cloves garlic, minced
- 1 tbsp olive oil
- 1 tbsp tomato paste
- Salt and black pepper, to taste
- 1 egg, beaten (for egg wash)

**Preparation instructions:**
1. Preheat the Air Fryer to 180°C for 5 minutes.
2. In a pan, heat olive oil and sauté chopped onion and garlic until softened.
3. Add shredded beef, Guinness beer, tomato paste, salt, and black pepper to the pan. Cook until the mixture thickens slightly.
4. Place a spoonful of the beef filling onto each puff pastry square.
5. Fold the pastry over the filling, sealing the edges with a fork. Brush the pie pockets with beaten egg for a golden finish.
6. Arrange the pie pockets in the air fryer basket.
7. Air fry at 180°C for 15 minutes or until the pastry turns golden brown and crispy.
8. Serve the Beef and Guinness Pie Pockets hot.

## Pork Belly Burnt Ends

Serves: 4
Prep time: 15 minutes / Cook time: 50 minutes

**Ingredients:**
- 600g pork belly, skin removed and cut into bite-sized cubes
- 2 tbsp barbecue rub or seasoning mix
- 60ml barbecue sauce
- 30g unsalted butter, melted
- 2 tbsp brown sugar
- Salt, to taste
- Wooden skewers, soaked in water

**Preparation instructions:**
1. Preheat the Air Fryer to 180°C for 5 minutes.
2. In a bowl, toss the pork belly cubes with barbecue rub and salt until evenly coated.
3. Thread the seasoned pork belly cubes onto soaked wooden skewers.
4. Place the skewers in the air fryer basket, ensuring they're not overcrowded.
5. Air fry at 180°C for 40-45 minutes, flipping the skewers halfway through the cooking time, until the pork belly is crispy and cooked through.
6. In a separate bowl, mix barbecue sauce, melted butter, and brown sugar.
7. Remove the skewers from the air fryer and brush the pork belly burnt ends with the barbecue sauce mixture.

8. Return the skewers to the air fryer and cook for an additional 5 minutes or until the sauce caramelizes slightly.
9. Once done, let the Pork Belly Burnt Ends rest for a few minutes before serving.

## Air Fried Lamb Kofta Kebabs with Mint Yoghurt Dip

Serves: 4
Prep time: 15 minutes / Cook time: 10 minutes

**Ingredients:**
- 500g ground lamb
- 1 small onion, finely chopped
- 2 cloves garlic, minced
- 2 tsp ground cumin
- 1 tsp ground coriander
- 1/2 tsp paprika
- Salt and black pepper, to taste
- Olive oil (for brushing)
- For Mint Yoghurt Dip:
- 150g Greek yoghurt
- 1 tbsp chopped fresh mint
- 1 tbsp lemon juice
- Salt, to taste

**Preparation instructions:**
1. Preheat the Air Fryer to 200°C for 5 minutes.
2. In a bowl, combine ground lamb, chopped onion, minced garlic, ground cumin, ground coriander, paprika, salt, and black pepper. Mix well and form into small kofta kebabs.
3. Brush the kofta kebabs with olive oil.
4. Place the kebabs in the air fryer basket in a single layer.
5. Air fry at 200°C for 8-10 minutes, turning them halfway through, until the kofta kebabs are cooked through and browned.
6. Meanwhile, prepare the Mint Yoghurt Dip by mixing Greek yoghurt, chopped fresh mint, lemon juice, and salt in a bowl. Refrigerate until serving.
7. Serve the Air Fried Lamb Kofta Kebabs hot with the Mint Yoghurt Dip.

## Spiced Beef Samosas

Makes: 12 samosas
Prep time: 30 minutes / Cook time: 12 minutes per batch

**Ingredients:**
- 300g minced beef
- 1 onion, finely chopped
- 2 cloves garlic, minced
- 1 tsp ground cumin
- 1 tsp ground coriander
- 1/2 tsp turmeric powder
- 1/2 tsp garam masala
- 1/4 tsp chili powder (adjust to taste)
- Salt, to taste
- 300g puff pastry, rolled and cut into rectangles
- 2 tbsp vegetable oil (for brushing)

**Preparation instructions:**
1. Preheat the Air Fryer to 180°C for 5 minutes.
2. In a pan, heat oil and sauté chopped onion and garlic until softened.
3. Add minced beef and cook until browned. Add ground cumin, ground coriander, turmeric powder, garam masala, chili powder, and salt. Mix well and cook for a few minutes. Remove from heat and let the mixture cool.
4. Cut the puff pastry into rectangles.
5. Take one rectangle and place a spoonful of the beef filling on one side.
6. Fold the pastry over the filling, forming a triangle. Seal the edges by pressing with a fork.
7. Brush the samosas with vegetable oil to coat lightly.
8. Place the samosas in the air fryer basket in a single layer.
9. Air fry at 180°C for 12 minutes per batch or until the samosas are golden brown and crispy.
10. Once done, remove the samosas from the air fryer and let them cool slightly before serving.

## Honey Glazed Air Fryer Pork Loin

Serves: 4
Prep time: 10 minutes / Cook time: 25 minutes

**Ingredients:**
- 600g pork loin, cut into thick slices
- 60ml honey
- 2 tbsp soy sauce
- 1 tbsp olive oil
- 2 cloves garlic, minced
- 1 tsp paprika
- Salt and black pepper, to taste
- Chopped fresh parsley, for garnish (optional)

**Preparation instructions:**
1. Preheat the Air Fryer to 180°C for 5 minutes.

2. In a bowl, mix honey, soy sauce, olive oil, minced garlic, paprika, salt, and black pepper.
3. Brush both sides of the pork loin slices generously with the honey glaze mixture.
4. Place the pork loin slices in the air fryer basket.
5. Air fry at 180°C for 20-25 minutes, flipping the slices halfway through the cooking time, until the pork reaches an internal temperature of 145°F (63°C) and the glaze caramelizes.
6. Once cooked, remove from the air fryer and let the pork loin rest for a few minutes before serving.
7. Optionally, garnish with chopped fresh parsley before serving.

## Air Fryer Beef Wellington Bites

Makes: 4 servings (approximately 12 bites)
Prep time: 30 minutes / Cook time: 20 minutes

**Ingredients:**
- 400g beef fillet or tenderloin, cut into 12 equal cubes
- 300g puff pastry, rolled and cut into small squares
- 2 tbsp Dijon mustard
- 200g mushroom duxelles (finely chopped mushrooms, cooked with garlic and herbs)
- 1 egg, beaten (for egg wash)
- Salt and black pepper, to taste

**Preparation instructions:**
1. Preheat the Air Fryer to 200°C for 5 minutes.
2. Season the beef fillet cubes with salt and black pepper.
3. Spread a little Dijon mustard on each beef cube.
4. Place a spoonful of mushroom duxelles on top of each beef cube with mustard.
5. Wrap each beef cube with puff pastry, sealing the edges by pressing gently.
6. Brush the wrapped beef Wellington bites with beaten egg for a golden finish.
7. Place the bites in the air fryer basket.
8. Air fry at 200°C for 18-20 minutes or until the puff pastry turns golden brown and the beef reaches your preferred level of doneness.
9. Once done, remove the Beef Wellington Bites from the air fryer and let them cool for a few minutes before serving.

## Garlic-Herb Crusted Air Fryer Rack of Lamb

Serves: 2-4
Prep time: 15 minutes / Cook time: 25 minutes

**Ingredients:**
- 600g rack of lamb, trimmed and frenched
- 2 cloves garlic, minced
- 2 tbsp fresh rosemary, finely chopped
- 2 tbsp fresh thyme, finely chopped
- 2 tbsp olive oil
- Salt and black pepper, to taste
- Dijon mustard (optional, for serving)

**Preparation instructions:**
1. Preheat the Air Fryer to 200°C for 5 minutes.
2. In a bowl, combine minced garlic, chopped rosemary, chopped thyme, olive oil, salt, and black pepper to create the herb crust.
3. Pat dry the rack of lamb and rub the herb crust mixture all over the lamb, coating it evenly.
4. Place the rack of lamb in the air fryer basket, fat-side up.
5. Air fry at 200°C for 20-25 minutes for medium-rare or adjust cooking time to your desired doneness, ensuring to check the internal temperature reaches 135-140°F (57-60°C) for medium-rare or 145°F (63°C) for medium.
6. Once cooked, remove the rack of lamb from the air fryer and let it rest for a few minutes before slicing. Serve with optional Dijon mustard on the side.

## Pork and Apple Stuffing Balls

Makes: 12 balls
Prep time: 20 minutes / Cook time: 15 minutes

**Ingredients:**
- 400g pork sausage meat
- 1 apple, peeled and finely diced
- 60g breadcrumbs
- 1 small onion, finely chopped
- 1 egg
- 1 tsp dried sage
- 1/2 tsp dried thyme
- Salt and black pepper, to taste
- Olive oil (for brushing)

**Preparation instructions:**
1. Preheat the Air Fryer to 180°C for 5 minutes.
2. In a bowl, mix together pork sausage meat, diced apple, breadcrumbs, chopped onion, egg, dried sage, dried thyme, salt, and black pepper until well combined.
3. Form the mixture into 12 balls and place them

on a plate.
4. Brush the pork and apple stuffing balls lightly with olive oil to help them brown.
5. Arrange the balls in the air fryer basket in a single layer.
6. Air fry at 180°C for 12-15 minutes or until the balls are cooked through and golden brown on the outside.
7. Once done, remove the stuffing balls from the air fryer and let them cool slightly before serving.

## Shepherd's Pie Stuffed Peppers

Serves: 4
Prep time: 20 minutes / Cook time: 25 minutes

**Ingredients:**
- 4 large bell peppers
- 400g minced lamb
- 1 onion, finely chopped
- 2 cloves garlic, minced
- 2 carrots, diced
- 200g frozen peas
- 400g mashed potatoes
- 60ml beef or vegetable broth
- 2 tbsp tomato paste
- 1 tbsp Worcestershire sauce
- 1 tsp dried thyme
- Salt and black pepper, to taste
- Chopped fresh parsley, for garnish (optional)

**Preparation instructions:**
1. Preheat the Air Fryer to 180°C for 5 minutes.
2. Cut the tops off the bell peppers and remove the seeds and membranes. Set aside.
3. In a pan, cook the minced lamb over medium heat until browned. Drain excess fat and set aside.
4. In the same pan, sauté chopped onion, minced garlic, and diced carrots until softened.
5. Add the browned lamb back to the pan, then stir in frozen peas, beef or vegetable broth, tomato paste, Worcestershire sauce, dried thyme, salt, and black pepper. Cook for a few more minutes.
6. Fill each bell pepper with the lamb and vegetable mixture.
7. Top each stuffed pepper with a layer of mashed potatoes.
8. Place the stuffed peppers in the air fryer basket.
9. Air fry at 180°C for 20-25 minutes or until the peppers are tender and the mashed potato topping is lightly browned.
10. Once cooked, garnish with chopped fresh parsley (if desired) before serving.

## Lamb and Apricot Skewers with Tzatziki

Serves: 4
Prep time: 15 minutes / Cook time: 10 minutes

**Ingredients:**
- 500g lamb leg steak, cubed
- 100g dried apricots, halved
- 2 tbsp olive oil
- 1 lemon, juiced
- 2 cloves garlic, minced
- 1 tsp ground cumin
- 1 tsp paprika
- Salt and black pepper, to taste
- Wooden skewers, soaked in water
- For Tzatziki:
- 150g Greek yoghurt
- 1/2 cucumber, grated and excess liquid squeezed out
- 1 clove garlic, minced
- 1 tbsp fresh lemon juice
- 1 tbsp chopped fresh mint or dill
- Salt and black pepper, to taste

**Preparation instructions:**
1. In a bowl, combine cubed lamb, halved dried apricots, olive oil, lemon juice, minced garlic, ground cumin, paprika, salt, and black pepper. Mix well and marinate for at least 1 hour in the refrigerator.
2. Preheat the Air Fryer to 200°C for 5 minutes.
3. Thread the marinated lamb and apricot alternately onto soaked wooden skewers.
4. Place the skewers in the air fryer basket.
5. Air fry at 200°C for 8-10 minutes, turning the skewers halfway through the cooking time, until the lamb is cooked to your desired doneness.
6. Meanwhile, prepare the Tzatziki by mixing Greek yoghurt, grated cucumber, minced garlic, lemon juice, chopped fresh mint or dill, salt, and black pepper in a bowl. Refrigerate until serving.
7. Serve the Lamb and Apricot Skewers hot with the prepared Tzatziki on the side.

# Sticky Maple Glazed Air Fryer Pork Ribs

Serves: 4
Prep time: 15 minutes / Cook time: 25 minutes

**Ingredients:**
- 800g pork ribs, cut into individual ribs
- 60ml maple syrup
- 2 tbsp soy sauce
- 2 tbsp apple cider vinegar
- 2 cloves garlic, minced
- 1 tsp smoked paprika
- 1/2 tsp ground ginger
- Salt and black pepper, to taste
- Sesame seeds and chopped spring onions, for garnish (optional)

**Preparation instructions:**
1. In a bowl, mix together maple syrup, soy sauce, apple cider vinegar, minced garlic, smoked paprika, ground ginger, salt, and black pepper to create the marinade.
2. Place the pork ribs in a resealable plastic bag or shallow dish and pour the marinade over them. Ensure the ribs are coated evenly. Marinate for at least 1-2 hours in the refrigerator.
3. Preheat the Air Fryer to 180°C for 5 minutes.
4. Remove the ribs from the marinade and place them in the air fryer basket in a single layer, reserving the marinade.
5. Air fry at 180°C for 20-25 minutes, turning the ribs halfway through, until they are cooked through and browned.
6. While the ribs are cooking, pour the reserved marinade into a small saucepan. Simmer over medium heat until it thickens into a glaze, stirring occasionally.
7. Once the ribs are done, brush the sticky maple glaze onto the ribs.
8. Optionally, garnish with sesame seeds and chopped spring onions before serving.

# Air Fried Beef and Mushroom Pies

Makes: 4 pies
Prep time: 20 minutes / Cook time: 20 minutes

**Ingredients:**
- 400g beef steak, diced
- 200g mushrooms, finely chopped
- 1 onion, finely chopped
- 2 cloves garlic, minced
- 250ml beef stock
- 1 tbsp Worcestershire sauce
- 1 tsp tomato paste
- 1 tsp dried thyme
- Salt and black pepper, to taste
- 400g puff pastry, rolled and cut into circles or squares
- 1 egg, beaten (for egg wash)

**Preparation instructions:**
1. Preheat the Air Fryer to 180°C for 5 minutes.
2. In a pan, heat some oil and cook diced beef until browned. Remove and set aside.
3. In the same pan, add chopped mushrooms, onion, and minced garlic. Cook until softened.
4. Return the browned beef to the pan. Add beef stock, Worcestershire sauce, tomato paste, dried thyme, salt, and black pepper. Simmer until the mixture thickens. Remove from heat and let it cool.
5. Cut the puff pastry into circles or squares, depending on the size of your pie dishes.
6. Place a spoonful of the beef and mushroom mixture into each pastry circle or square.
7. Fold the pastry over the filling, sealing the edges by pressing with a fork. Brush the pies with beaten egg.
8. Place the pies in the air fryer basket.
9. Air fry at 180°C for 15-20 minutes or until the pastry is golden brown and cooked through.
10. Once done, remove the beef and mushroom pies from the air fryer and let them cool slightly before serving.

# Asian Style Air Fryer Beef Stir-Fry

Servings: 2
Prep time: 28 minutes / Cook Time: 6 minutes

**Ingredients:**
- 350 g beef steak (such as sirloin or flank), thinly sliced
- 2 tablespoons soy sauce
- 1 tablespoon oyster sauce
- 1 tablespoon hoisin sauce
- 1 tablespoon rice vinegar
- 2 teaspoons sesame oil

- 2 teaspoons cornstarch
- 1 teaspoon grated ginger
- 2 cloves garlic, minced
- 1 Yellow, Red and Green bell pepper each, thinly sliced
- 1 medium onion, thinly sliced
- 100g snap peas
- 1 tablespoon vegetable oil
- Optional garnish: sliced green onions and sesame seeds

**Preparation instructions:**
1. Mix the soy sauce, oyster sauce, hoisin sauce, rice vinegar, sesame oil, cornstarch, grated ginger, and minced garlic in a bowl. Stir well to create a marinade for the beef.
2. Add the thinly sliced beef to the marinade and toss until all the slices are well coated. Let the beef marinate for at least 20 minutes, soaking up the flavors.
3. Preheat your air fryer to 200°C for a few minutes.
4. While the air fryer heats up, heat the vegetable oil in a large skillet or wok over medium-high heat. Add the bell peppers, onion, and snap peas, and stir-fry for 3-4 minutes until they soften. Remove the vegetables from the skillet and set them aside.
5. Add the marinated beef slices in the same skillet and cook for 3-4 minutes. Make sure to discard any excess marinade.
6. Transfer the cooked beef to the preheated air fryer basket, spreading it in a single layer. Cook for 5-6 minutes, shaking the basket or flipping the beef halfway through, until the beef is crispy and browned.
7. Return the cooked vegetables to the skillet with the beef and toss them together for a minute to combine and reheat.
8. Once the beef and vegetables are thoroughly combined, remove from heat and serve the Asian style stir-fry immediately.
9. If desired, you can garnish your stir fry with sliced green onions and sesame seeds.

## BBQ Rubbed Air Fryer Pork Ribs

Servings: 2
Prep time: 5 minutes / Cook Time: 35 minutes

**Ingredients:**
- 800 g pork ribs
- 60 g brown sugar
- 15 g smoked paprika
- 15 g garlic powder
- 10 g onion powder
- 5 g salt
- 5 g black pepper
- 30 ml olive oil
- BBQ sauce for serving

**Preparation instructions:**
1. Preheat your Ninja Dual Zone air fryer to 180°C.
2. Combine the brown sugar, smoked paprika, garlic powder, onion powder, salt, and black pepper in a bowl to make the BBQ rub.
3. Rub the olive oil all over the pork ribs to help the rub stick.
4. Generously coat the pork ribs with the BBQ rub, ensuring that both sides are well-covered.
5. Place the ribs in the air fryer basket, ensuring they are not overcrowded.
6. Air fry the ribs for 30-35 minutes, flipping them halfway through cooking.
7. Once the ribs are cooked and tender, remove them from the air fryer.
8. Let the ribs rest for a few minutes, then serve hot with additional BBQ sauce on the side.

## Smoked Pork Ribs

Serves 7
Prep time: 5 minutes / Cook time: 20 minutes

**Ingredients:**
- 20 pork ribs (2 racks)
- 600g BBQ sauce
- 2 tsp liquid smoke
- 2 tsp sea salt
- 1 tsp black pepper, grounded

**Preparation instructions:**
1. Place the pork ribs in a large mixing bowl and dash in the salt, pepper and liquid smoke, then leave the ribs for 5 minutes
2. Follow this by drenching the pork ribs in ¾ of the BBQ sauce and then rub it in
3. Place the 10 ribs in each draws on the dual zone
4. Pair the dual zone to 'ROAST' at 200°C for 20 minutes, then press 'MATCH' and 'STOP/START' to smoke the pork ribs
5. At the 6 minute mark of cooking flip the pork

ribs and baste the remainder of the BBQ sauce
6. Once complete, retrieve the smoked pork ribs to serve

## Chuck Kebab with Rocket

Serves 4
Prep time: 30 minutes / Cook time: 25 minutes

**Ingredients:**
- 120 ml leeks, chopped
- 2 garlic cloves, smashed
- 900 g beef mince
- Salt, to taste
- ¼ teaspoon ground black pepper, or more to taste
- 1 teaspoon cayenne pepper
- ½ teaspoon ground sumac
- 3 saffron threads
- 2 tablespoons loosely packed fresh flat-leaf parsley leaves
- 4 tablespoons tahini sauce
- 110 g baby rocket
- 1 tomato, cut into slices

**Preparation instructions:**
1. In a bowl, mix the chopped leeks, garlic, beef mince, and spices; knead with your hands until everything is well incorporated.
2. Now, mound the beef mixture around a wooden skewer into a pointed-ended sausage.
3. Cook in the preheated air fryer at 182°C for 25 minutes. Serve your kebab with the tahini sauce, baby rocket and tomato. Enjoy!

## Italian Lamb Chops with Avocado Mayo

Serves 2
Prep time: 5 minutes / Cook time: 12 minutes

**Ingredients:**
- 2 lamp chops
- 2 teaspoons Italian herbs
- 2 avocados
- 120 ml mayonnaise
- 1 tablespoon lemon juice

**Preparation instructions:**
1. Season the lamb chops with the Italian herbs, then set aside for 5 minutes.
2. Preheat the air fryer to 204°C and place the rack inside.
3. Put the chops on the rack and air fry for 12 minutes.
4. In the meantime, halve the avocados and open to remove the pits. Spoon the flesh into a blender.
5. Add the mayonnaise and lemon juice and pulse until a smooth consistency is achieved.
6. Take care when removing the chops from the air fryer, then plate up and serve with the avocado mayo.

## Spicy Rump Steak

Serves 4
Prep time: 25 minutes / Cook time: 12-18 minutes

**Ingredients:**
- 2 tablespoons salsa
- 1 tablespoon minced chipotle pepper or chipotle paste
- 1 tablespoon apple cider vinegar
- 1 teaspoon ground cumin
- ⅛ teaspoon freshly ground black pepper
- ⅛ teaspoon red pepper flakes
- 340 g rump steak, cut into 4 pieces and gently pounded to about ⅓ inch thick
- Cooking oil spray

**Preparation instructions:**
1. In a small bowl, thoroughly mix the salsa, chipotle pepper, vinegar, cumin, black pepper, and red pepper flakes. Rub this mixture into both sides of each steak piece. Let stand for 15 minutes at room temperature.
2. Insert the crisper plate into the basket and place the basket into the unit. Preheat the unit by selecting AIR FRY, setting the temperature to 200°C, and setting the time to 3 minutes. Select START/STOP to begin.
3. Once the unit is preheated, spray the crisper plate with cooking oil. Working in batches, place 2 steaks into the basket.
4. Select AIR FRY, set the temperature to 200°C, and set the time to 9 minutes. Select START/STOP to begin.
5. After about 6 minutes, check the steaks. If a food thermometer inserted into the meat registers at least 64°C, they are done. If not, resume cooking.
6. When the cooking is done, transfer the steaks to a clean plate and cover with aluminum foil to keep warm. Repeat steps 3, 4, and 5 with the remaining steaks.
7. Thinly slice the steaks against the grain and serve.

# Chapter 5: Fish And Seafood

## Air Fryer Lemon-Herb Crusted Cod Fillets

Serves: 4
Prep time: 15 minutes / Cook time: 12 minutes

**Ingredients:**
- 4 cod fillets (about 150g each)
- Zest of 1 lemon
- 2 tbsp fresh parsley, chopped
- 1 tbsp fresh dill, chopped
- 60g breadcrumbs
- 2 tbsp olive oil
- Salt and black pepper, to taste
- Lemon wedges, for serving

**Preparation instructions:**
1. Preheat the Air Fryer to 200°C for 5 minutes.
2. In a bowl, combine lemon zest, chopped parsley, chopped dill, breadcrumbs, olive oil, salt, and black pepper to create the herb crust.
3. Pat dry the cod fillets and coat them evenly with the herb crust mixture.
4. Place the cod fillets in the air fryer basket.
5. Air fry at 200°C for 10-12 minutes or until the cod is cooked through and the crust is golden brown.
6. Once cooked, remove from the air fryer and serve with lemon wedges.

## Panko-Crusted Air Fried Scallops

Serves: 4
Prep time: 15 minutes / Cook time: 8 minutes

**Ingredients:**
- 400g scallops, patted dry
- 60g panko breadcrumbs
- 2 tbsp grated Parmesan cheese
- 1 tsp smoked paprika
- 1/2 tsp garlic powder
- 1/4 tsp onion powder
- 1 egg, beaten
- Salt and black pepper, to taste
- Cooking spray or olive oil spray

**Preparation instructions:**
1. Preheat the Air Fryer to 200°C for 5 minutes.
2. In a shallow dish, mix together panko breadcrumbs, grated Parmesan cheese, smoked paprika, garlic powder, onion powder, salt, and black pepper.
3. Dip each scallop in beaten egg, then coat evenly with the panko mixture, pressing gently to adhere.
4. Lightly coat the air fryer basket with cooking spray or brush with olive oil.
5. Place the coated scallops in the air fryer basket in a single layer.
6. Air fry at 200°C for 6-8 minutes or until the scallops are golden brown and cooked through, flipping them halfway through the cooking time.
7. Once done, remove the scallops from the air fryer and serve immediately.

## Smoked Paprika Air Fryer Prawns

Serves: 4
Prep time: 10 minutes / Cook time: 6 minutes

**Ingredients:**
- 500g large prawns, peeled and deveined
- 2 tbsp olive oil
- 1 tsp smoked paprika
- 1/2 tsp garlic powder
- 1/2 tsp onion powder
- Salt and black pepper, to taste
- Lemon wedges, for serving

**Preparation instructions:**
1. Preheat the Air Fryer to 200°C for 5 minutes.
2. In a bowl, toss the prawns with olive oil, smoked paprika, garlic powder, onion powder, salt, and black pepper until evenly coated.
3. Place the seasoned prawns in the air fryer basket.
4. Air fry at 200°C for 5-6 minutes, shaking the basket halfway through the cooking time, until the prawns are pink and cooked through.
5. Once cooked, remove the prawns from the air fryer and serve with lemon wedges.

## Air Fried Garlic Butter Lobster Tails

Serves: 4
Prep time: 15 minutes / Cook time: 10 minutes

**Ingredients:**
- 4 lobster tails
- 100g unsalted butter, melted
- 4 cloves garlic, minced
- 2 tbsp chopped fresh parsley
- Salt and black pepper, to taste
- Lemon wedges, for serving

**Preparation instructions:**
1. Preheat the Air Fryer to 200°C for 5 minutes.
2. Use kitchen shears to cut the top shell of each lobster tail down to the tail.
3. Gently pull the meat away from the shell, leaving it attached at the base.
4. In a bowl, mix melted butter, minced garlic, chopped parsley, salt, and black pepper.
5. Brush the lobster tails generously with the garlic butter mixture.
6. Place the lobster tails in the air fryer basket, shell-side down.
7. Air fry at 200°C for 8-10 minutes until the lobster meat is opaque and cooked through.
8. Once done, remove from the air fryer and serve with lemon wedges.

## Crispy Coconut-Crusted Air Fryer Haddock

Serves: 4
Prep time: 15 minutes / Cook time: 10 minutes

**Ingredients:**
- 4 haddock fillets
- 50g shredded coconut
- 50g breadcrumbs
- 1 egg, beaten
- 2 tbsp plain flour
- 1 tsp paprika
- 1/2 tsp garlic powder
- Salt and black pepper, to taste
- Cooking spray or olive oil spray

**Preparation instructions:**
1. Preheat the Air Fryer to 200°C for 5 minutes.
2. In one bowl, mix shredded coconut and breadcrumbs.
3. In another bowl, combine plain flour, paprika, garlic powder, salt, and black pepper.
4. Pat dry the haddock fillets. Dip each fillet first in the seasoned flour, then in the beaten egg, and finally coat with the coconut-breadcrumb mixture.
5. Lightly coat the air fryer basket with cooking spray or brush with olive oil.
6. Place the coated haddock fillets in the air fryer basket.
7. Air fry at 200°C for 8-10 minutes until the coating is crispy and the fish is cooked through.
8. Once cooked, remove from the air fryer and serve immediately.

## Sea Bass with Mediterranean Herbs

Serves: 4
Prep time: 15 minutes / Cook time: 12 minutes

**Ingredients:**
- 4 sea bass fillets
- 2 tbsp olive oil
- 2 cloves garlic, minced
- 1 tsp dried oregano
- 1 tsp dried thyme
- 1 tsp dried rosemary
- Salt and black pepper, to taste
- Lemon wedges, for serving

**Preparation instructions:**
1. Preheat the Air Fryer to 190°C for 5 minutes.
2. In a small bowl, mix together olive oil, minced garlic, dried oregano, dried thyme, dried rosemary, salt, and black pepper.
3. Pat dry the sea bass fillets and brush them with the herb-infused oil mixture.
4. Place the sea bass fillets in the air fryer basket.
5. Air fry at 190°C for 10-12 minutes until the fish is cooked through and flakes easily with a fork.
6. Once done, remove from the air fryer and serve with lemon wedges.

## Lemon-Dill Air Fryer Salmon Patties

Serves: 4
Prep time: 15 minutes / Cook time: 10 minutes

**Ingredients:**
- 400g salmon fillet, cooked and flaked
- Zest of 1 lemon
- 2 tbsp chopped fresh dill
- 50g breadcrumbs
- 1 egg, beaten

- 2 tbsp mayonnaise
- 1/2 tsp garlic powder
- Salt and black pepper, to taste
- Cooking spray or olive oil spray

**Preparation instructions:**
1. Preheat the Air Fryer to 180°C for 5 minutes.
2. In a bowl, combine cooked and flaked salmon, lemon zest, chopped fresh dill, breadcrumbs, beaten egg, mayonnaise, garlic powder, salt, and black pepper.
3. Mix until well combined and shape the mixture into 4 patties.
4. Lightly coat the air fryer basket with cooking spray or brush with olive oil.
5. Place the salmon patties in the air fryer basket.
6. Air fry at 180°C for 8-10 minutes, flipping halfway through, until the patties are golden brown and cooked through.
7. Once done, remove from the air fryer and serve.

## Tempura-style Air Fried King Prawns

Serves: 4
Prep time: 15 minutes / Cook time: 8 minutes

**Ingredients:**
- 300g king prawns, peeled and deveined
- 100g plain flour
- 50g cornflour
- 1/2 tsp baking powder
- 150ml ice-cold water
- Salt, to taste
- Dipping sauce of your choice (e.g., sweet chili sauce)

**Preparation instructions:**
1. Preheat the Air Fryer to 200°C for 5 minutes.
2. In a bowl, mix plain flour, cornflour, baking powder, and a pinch of salt.
3. Gradually add ice-cold water to the dry Ingredients:, whisking until the batter is smooth.
4. Dip the king prawns into the batter to coat them evenly.
5. Lightly coat the air fryer basket with cooking spray or brush with olive oil.
6. Place the battered king prawns in the air fryer basket.
7. Air fry at 200°C for 6-8 minutes until the prawns are golden and crispy.
8. Once done, remove from the air fryer and serve with your preferred dipping sauce.

## Air Fryer Cajun Tilapia

Serves: 4
Prep time: 10 minutes / Cook time: 10 minutes

**Ingredients:**
- 4 tilapia fillets
- 2 tbsp olive oil
- 1 tbsp Cajun seasoning
- 1/2 tsp garlic powder
- 1/2 tsp onion powder
- 1/2 tsp paprika
- 1/2 tsp dried thyme
- Salt and black pepper, to taste
- Lemon wedges, for serving

**Preparation instructions:**
1. Preheat the Air Fryer to 200°C for 5 minutes.
2. In a bowl, mix together olive oil, Cajun seasoning, garlic powder, onion powder, paprika, dried thyme, salt, and black pepper to make the marinade.
3. Pat dry the tilapia fillets and rub them with the Cajun marinade, ensuring they are evenly coated. Let them marinate for at least 15 minutes.
4. Lightly coat the air fryer basket with cooking spray or brush with olive oil.
5. Place the marinated tilapia fillets in the air fryer basket.
6. Air fry at 200°C for 8-10 minutes until the fish is cooked through and flakes easily with a fork.
7. Once done, remove from the air fryer and serve with lemon wedges.

## Garlic and Parmesan Crusted Air Fryer Mussels

Serves: 4
Prep time: 15 minutes / Cook time: 8 minutes

**Ingredients:**
- 800g fresh mussels, cleaned and debearded
- 50g grated Parmesan cheese
- 3 cloves garlic, minced
- 2 tbsp fresh parsley, chopped
- 50g breadcrumbs

- 2 tbsp olive oil
- Salt and black pepper, to taste
- Lemon wedges, for serving

**Preparation instructions:**
1. Preheat the Air Fryer to 200°C for 5 minutes.
2. In a bowl, combine grated Parmesan cheese, minced garlic, chopped fresh parsley, breadcrumbs, olive oil, salt, and black pepper.
3. Pat dry the cleaned mussels and discard any that are open or damaged.
4. Coat each mussel with the Parmesan-garlic mixture.
5. Place the coated mussels in the air fryer basket.
6. Air fry at 200°C for 6-8 minutes until the crust is golden and the mussels are cooked.
7. Once done, remove from the air fryer and serve with lemon wedges.

## Tandoori Marinated Air Fryer Monkfish

Serves: 4
Prep time: 20 minutes / Cook time: 12 minutes

**Ingredients:**
- 600g monkfish fillets, cut into chunks
- 4 tbsp Greek yoghurt
- 2 tbsp tandoori paste
- 1 tbsp lemon juice
- 1 tsp ground cumin
- 1 tsp ground coriander
- 1/2 tsp turmeric
- 1/2 tsp paprika
- Salt, to taste
- Cooking spray or olive oil spray
- Fresh coriander leaves, for garnish

**Preparation instructions:**
1. In a bowl, mix Greek yoghurt, tandoori paste, lemon juice, ground cumin, ground coriander, turmeric, paprika, and salt to form the marinade.
2. Coat the monkfish chunks with the marinade and let them marinate for at least 1 hour in the refrigerator.
3. Preheat the Air Fryer to 200°C for 5 minutes.
4. Lightly coat the air fryer basket with cooking spray or brush with olive oil.
5. Place the marinated monkfish in the air fryer basket.
6. Air fry at 200°C for 10-12 minutes until the monkfish is cooked through and lightly charred.
7. Once done, remove from the air fryer and garnish with fresh coriander leaves before serving.

## Crispy Salt and Pepper Squid

Serves: 4
Prep time: 15 minutes / Cook time: 8 minutes

**Ingredients:**
- 500g squid tubes, cleaned and sliced into rings
- 50g cornflour
- 50g plain flour
- 1 tsp sea salt
- 1 tsp ground black pepper
- 1/2 tsp paprika
- Cooking spray or olive oil spray
- Lemon wedges, for serving

**Preparation instructions:**
1. In a bowl, mix cornflour, plain flour, sea salt, black pepper, and paprika.
2. Coat the squid rings in the flour mixture, shaking off excess flour.
3. Preheat the Air Fryer to 200°C for 5 minutes.
4. Lightly coat the air fryer basket with cooking spray or brush with olive oil.
5. Place the coated squid rings in the air fryer basket in a single layer.
6. Air fry at 200°C for 6-8 minutes until the squid is crispy and lightly golden.
7. Once done, remove from the air fryer and serve with lemon wedges.

## Grilled Garlic and Herb King Prawns

Serves: 4
Prep time: 15 minutes / Cook time: 5 minutes

**Ingredients:**
- 500g king prawns, peeled and deveined
- 3 cloves garlic, minced
- 2 tablespoons fresh parsley, chopped
- 2 tablespoons fresh dill, chopped
- 2 tablespoons olive oil
- 1 tablespoon lemon juice
- Salt and pepper to taste

**Preparation instructions:**
1. In a bowl, combine the minced garlic, chopped fresh parsley, chopped fresh dill, olive oil, lemon juice, salt, and pepper. Mix well to create a marinade.
2. Add the king prawns to the marinade and toss to coat them evenly. Allow the prawns to marinate for about 10 minutes.
3. Preheat a grill or grill pan over medium-high heat.
4. Thread the marinated prawns onto skewers, leaving a little space between each prawn.
5. Grill the prawns for about 2-3 minutes per side, or until they turn pink and opaque. Be careful not to overcook them as they can become tough.
6. Once cooked, remove the prawns from the skewers and transfer them to a serving plate.

## Creamy Garlic Butter Mussels

Serves: 4
Prep time: 15 minutes / Cook time: 10 minutes

**Ingredients:**
- 1000g fresh mussels, cleaned and debearded
- 30g butter
- 4 cloves garlic, minced
- 120ml white wine
- 120ml heavy cream
- 2 tablespoons fresh parsley, chopped
- Salt and pepper to taste
- Fresh lemon wedges, for serving
- Crusty bread, for serving

**Preparation instructions:**
1. Heat butter in a large pot or skillet over medium heat. Add the minced garlic and sauté for about 1 minute until fragrant.
2. Add the cleaned and debearded mussels to the pot. Pour in the white wine and cover the pot with a lid. Steam the mussels for about 4-5 minutes, or until they open up. Discard any mussels that remain closed after cooking.
3. Using a slotted spoon, transfer the cooked mussels to a serving bowl, leaving the cooking liquid in the pot.
4. Pour the heavy cream into the pot with the cooking liquid. Stir well and let it simmer for a few minutes until the sauce slightly thickens.
5. Season the sauce with salt, pepper, and chopped fresh parsley. Stir to combine.
6. Pour the creamy garlic butter sauce over the cooked mussels in the serving bowl.
7. Serve the creamy garlic butter mussels hot, accompanied by fresh lemon wedges and crusty bread. They make a delightful seafood dish that can be enjoyed as an appetiser or as a main course.

## Southern-Style Catfish

Serves 4
Prep time: 10 minutes / Cook time: 12 minutes

- 4 (200 g) catfish fillets
- 80 ml heavy whipping cream
- 1 tablespoon lemon juice
- 110 g blanched finely ground almond flour
- 2 teaspoons Old Bay seasoning
- ½ teaspoon salt
- ¼ teaspoon ground black pepper

**Preparation instructions:**
1. Place catfish fillets into a large bowl with cream and pour in lemon juice. Stir to coat.
2. In a separate large bowl, mix flour and Old Bay seasoning.
3. Remove each fillet and gently shake off excess cream. Sprinkle with salt and pepper. Press each fillet gently into flour mixture on both sides to coat.
4. Place fillets into ungreased air fryer basket. Adjust the temperature to 204°C and air fry for 12 minutes, turning fillets halfway through cooking. Catfish will be golden brown and have an internal temperature of at least 64°C when done. Serve warm.

## Coconut Cream Mackerel

Serves 4
Prep time: 10 minutes / Cook time: 6 minutes

**Ingredients:**
- 900 g mackerel fillet
- 240 ml coconut cream
- 1 teaspoon ground coriander
- 1 teaspoon cumin seeds
- 1 garlic clove, peeled, chopped

**Preparation instructions:**
1. Chop the mackerel roughly and sprinkle it with coconut cream, ground coriander, cumin seeds,

and garlic.

2. Then put the fish in the air fryer and cook at 204ºC for 6 minutes.

## Mediterranean Grilled Whole Fish

Servings: 2
Prep time: 10 minutes / Cook Time: 10 minutes

**Ingredients:**
- 1 whole fish (such as sea bass, snapper, or trout), cleaned and scaled (approximately 600-800 grams)
- 30 ml olive oil
- 15 ml lemon juice
- 2 cloves garlic, minced
- Dried oregano
- Dried thyme
- Paprika
- Salt
- Black pepper
- Fresh herbs (such as parsley or basil), for garnish
- Lemon slices (for serving)

**Preparation instructions:**
1. Preheat your Air Fryer to 150C.
2. Rinse the whole fish under cold water and pat it dry with paper towels.
3. Mix the olive oil, lemon juice, minced garlic, dried oregano, dried thyme, paprika, salt, and black pepper in a bowl to create the Mediterranean marinade.
4. Make diagonal cuts on both sides of the fish, about 1 inch apart. This will help the marinade penetrate the fish and ensure even cooking.
5. Brush the fish inside and out with the Mediterranean marinade, ensuring it is evenly coated. Reserve a small amount of the marinade for basting during air frying.
6. Place the fish in your preheated Air Fryer drawer, close it, and grill for approximately 4-5 minutes per side, or until the flesh is opaque and flakes easily with a fork.
7. While grilling in your Air fryer, occasionally baste the fish with the reserved marinade to keep it moist and flavorful.
8. Carefully remove the grilled whole fish and transfer it to a serving platter.
9. Serve the Mediterranean grilled whole fish hot, along with a side of roasted vegetables.

## Lemon Garlic Shrimp Skewers

Servings: 2
Prep time: 30 minutes / Cook Time: 20 minutes

**Ingredients:**
- 300 grams of shrimp, peeled and deveined
- 1 lemon
- 2 cloves of garlic
- 20 ml of olive oil
- Salt and pepper to taste
- Wooden skewers

**Preparation instructions:**
1. Soak the wooden skewers in water for about 20 minutes to prevent them from burning in the air dryer.
2. In a mixing bowl, combine the juice of one lemon, minced garlic, olive oil, salt, and pepper. Stir well to make a marinade.
3. Add the shrimp to the marinade and toss to coat them evenly. Let them marinate for at least 15 minutes to allow the flavors to meld.
4. Preheat your Ninja Dual Zone Air Fryer to 170C.
5. Thread the marinated shrimp onto the soaked wooden skewers, dividing them evenly.
6. Place the shrimp skewers in the drawers of your preheated air fryer and cook for about 2-3 minutes per side, or until they turn pink and opaque.
7. While grilling, brush the remaining lemon juice over the shrimp skewers for extra flavor.
8. Remove the skewers from the grill and transfer them to a serving platter.
9. Garnish with freshly chopped parsley and serve hot as an appetizer or main course.

## Bang Bang Shrimp

Servings: 2
Prep time: 30 minutes / Cook Time: 20 minutes

**Ingredients:**
- 250 grams shrimp, peeled and deveined
- 3 tablespoons mayonnaise
- 1 tablespoon sweet chili sauce
- 1 tablespoon Sriracha sauce
- 1 teaspoon honey
- 1 teaspoon lime juice

- 1 clove garlic, minced
- Salt, to taste
- Vegetable oil, for frying
- Green onions, sliced (for garnish)

**Preparation instructions:**

1. Combine the mayonnaise, sweet chili sauce, Sriracha sauce, honey, lime juice, minced garlic, and a pinch of salt in a small bowl. Mix well to create the bang bang sauce. Set it aside.
2. Preheat your Ninja Dual Zone Air Fryer to a temperature of 200C. Make sure there is enough oil to fully submerge the shrimp.
3. Rinse the shrimp under cold water and pat them dry with a paper towel. Season them with salt.
4. Lightly spray the air fryer basket with vegetable oil to prevent sticking. Place half of the coated shrimp in one zone of the air fryer basket and the remaining shrimp in the other zone. Make sure they are evenly spaced and not touching each other.
5. Close the air fryer lid and set the timer for 8 minutes. After 4 minutes, open the lid and flip the shrimp to ensure even cooking.
6. Toss the fried shrimp in a large bowl with the prepared bang bang sauce, ensuring each piece is coated evenly.
7. Transfer the bang bang shrimp to a serving plate and garnish with sliced green onions for freshness and presentation.

## Grilled Garlic Butter Lobster Tails

Servings: 2
Prep time: 120 minutes / Cook Time: 6 minutes

**Ingredients:**

- 2 lobster tails
- 60 grams butter, melted
- 2 cloves garlic, minced
- 1 tablespoon fresh lemon juice
- Salt, to taste
- Black pepper, to taste
- Cooking spray or oil (for grilling)
- Fresh parsley, chopped (for garnish)
- Lemon wedges (for serving)

**Preparation instructions:**

1. Preheat the Ninja Dual Zone Air Fryer to Grill mode.
2. Using kitchen shears or a sharp knife, carefully cut through the top shell of each lobster tail lengthwise, stopping at the tail. Gently spread the shell apart to expose the meat.
3. Combine the melted butter, minced garlic, lemon juice, salt, and black pepper in a small bowl. Mix well to create the garlic butter sauce.
4. Brush the lobster tails generously with the garlic butter sauce, coating the meat thoroughly.
5. Lightly coat the non stick plates of the Ninja Dual Zone Air Fryer with cooking spray or brush it with a little oil to prevent sticking.
6. Place the lobster tails on the non stick plates, meat side down, and close the lid.
7. Grill the lobster tails in the first zone for 4-5 minutes. While the first zone is grilling, preheat the second zone to Grill Mode.
8. After 4-5 minutes, open the lid and flip the lobster tails using tongs or a spatula. Brush the exposed side with more garlic butter sauce.
9. Close the lid and grill the lobster tails in the second zone for 4-5 minutes, or until the meat is opaque and firm.
10. Once grilled to perfection, remove the lobster tails from the Ninja Dual Zone Air Fryer and transfer them to a serving platter.
11. Garnish the lobster tails with freshly chopped parsley for added freshness and presentation.
12. Serve the grilled garlic butter lobster tails immediately. You can enjoy it with lemon wedges on the side.

# Chapter 6: Sides & Appetisers

## Air Fryer Garlic Parmesan Courgette Chips

Serves: 4
Prep time: 15 minutes / Cook time: 10 minutes

**Ingredients:**
- 2 large courgettes (zucchinis), sliced into thin rounds
- 50g grated Parmesan cheese
- 2 tbsp olive oil
- 2 cloves garlic, minced
- 1/2 tsp garlic powder
- Salt and black pepper, to taste
- Cooking spray or olive oil spray

**Preparation instructions:**
1. Preheat the Air Fryer to 200°C for 5 minutes.
2. In a bowl, toss the courgette rounds with olive oil, minced garlic, garlic powder, salt, and black pepper until evenly coated.
3. In a separate bowl, combine the grated Parmesan cheese.
4. Dip each courgette round into the Parmesan cheese, pressing gently to coat.
5. Lightly coat the air fryer basket with cooking spray or brush with olive oil.
6. Place the coated courgette rounds in the air fryer basket in a single layer.
7. Air fry at 200°C for 8-10 minutes until the chips are golden brown and crispy.
8. Once done, remove from the air fryer and serve immediately.

## Crispy Air Fried Halloumi Fries

Serves: 4
Prep time: 10 minutes / Cook time: 8 minutes

**Ingredients:**
- 250g halloumi cheese, cut into fries
- 50g plain flour
- 2 eggs, beaten
- 100g breadcrumbs
- 1 tsp smoked paprika
- Cooking spray or olive oil spray
- Lemon wedges, for serving

**Preparation instructions:**
1. Preheat the Air Fryer to 200°C for 5 minutes.
2. Place the plain flour, beaten eggs, and breadcrumbs mixed with smoked paprika in three separate bowls.
3. Dip each halloumi fry first in the flour, then in the beaten egg, and finally coat with the breadcrumb mixture.
4. Lightly coat the air fryer basket with cooking spray or brush with olive oil.
5. Place the coated halloumi fries in the air fryer basket.
6. Air fry at 200°C for 6-8 minutes until the fries are golden and crispy.
7. Once done, remove from the air fryer and serve with lemon wedges.

## Pesto-Stuffed Air Fryer Mushrooms

Serves: 4
Prep time: 15 minutes / Cook time: 12 minutes

**Ingredients:**
- 8 large button mushrooms, stems removed
- 4 tbsp pesto
- 50g breadcrumbs
- 30g grated Parmesan cheese
- Cooking spray or olive oil spray

**Preparation instructions:**
1. Preheat the Air Fryer to 180°C for 5 minutes.
2. In a bowl, mix together the breadcrumbs and grated Parmesan cheese.
3. Stuff each mushroom cap with a tablespoon of pesto and press the breadcrumb mixture on top.
4. Lightly coat the air fryer basket with cooking spray or brush with olive oil.
5. Place the stuffed mushrooms in the air fryer basket.
6. Air fry at 180°C for 10-12 minutes until the mushrooms are tender and the topping is golden.
7. Once done, remove from the air fryer and serve.

## Air Fried Sweet Potato Wedges with Rosemary

Serves: 4
Prep time: 15 minutes / Cook time: 20 minutes

**Ingredients:**
- 600g sweet potatoes, cut into wedges
- 2 tbsp olive oil
- 1 tbsp fresh rosemary, chopped
- 1/2 tsp garlic powder
- Salt and black pepper, to taste

**Preparation instructions:**
1. Preheat the Air Fryer to 200°C for 5 minutes.
2. In a bowl, toss the sweet potato wedges with olive oil, chopped rosemary, garlic powder, salt, and black pepper until evenly coated.
3. Lightly coat the air fryer basket with cooking spray or brush with olive oil.
4. Place the sweet potato wedges in the air fryer basket in a single layer.
5. Air fry at 200°C for 18-20 minutes, shaking the basket halfway through, until the wedges are crispy and golden.
6. Once done, remove from the air fryer and serve hot.

## Tempura-style Air Fryer Green Beans

Serves: 4
Prep time: 10 minutes / Cook time: 8 minutes

**Ingredients:**
- 300g fresh green beans, trimmed
- 100g plain flour
- 1/4 tsp baking powder
- 1/4 tsp salt
- 150ml ice-cold water
- Cooking spray or olive oil spray
- Dipping sauce of your choice

**Preparation instructions:**
1. Preheat the Air Fryer to 200°C for 5 minutes.
2. In a bowl, whisk together plain flour, baking powder, salt, and ice-cold water until the batter is smooth.
3. Dip the green beans into the batter, allowing any excess batter to drip off.
4. Lightly coat the air fryer basket with cooking spray or brush with olive oil.
5. Place the coated green beans in the air fryer basket.
6. Air fry at 200°C for 6-8 minutes until the green beans are crispy and lightly golden.
7. Once done, remove from the air fryer and serve with your preferred dipping sauce.

## Stuffed Jalapeño Peppers with Cream Cheese

Serves: 4
Prep time: 15 minutes / Cook time: 12 minutes

**Ingredients:**
- 8 large jalapeño peppers
- 100g cream cheese, softened
- 50g shredded cheddar cheese
- 2 spring onions, finely chopped
- 1/2 tsp garlic powder
- Salt and black pepper, to taste

**Preparation instructions:**
1. Preheat the Air Fryer to 180°C for 5 minutes.
2. Cut each jalapeño pepper in half lengthwise and remove the seeds and membranes.
3. In a bowl, mix together the softened cream cheese, shredded cheddar cheese, chopped spring onions, garlic powder, salt, and black pepper.
4. Fill each jalapeño half with the cream cheese mixture.
5. Lightly coat the air fryer basket with cooking spray or brush with olive oil.
6. Place the stuffed jalapeño peppers in the air fryer basket.
7. Air fry at 180°C for 10-12 minutes until the peppers are tender and the cheese is melted and lightly browned.
8. Once done, remove from the air fryer and let cool for a few minutes before serving.

## Air Fryer Balsamic Glazed Brussels Sprouts

Serves: 4
Prep time: 10 minutes / Cook time: 15 minutes

**Ingredients:**
- 500g Brussels sprouts, trimmed and halved
- 2 tbsp olive oil
- 2 tbsp balsamic vinegar

- 1 tbsp honey or maple syrup
- Salt and black pepper, to taste

**Preparation instructions:**
1. Preheat the Air Fryer to 200°C for 5 minutes.
2. In a bowl, toss Brussels sprouts with olive oil, balsamic vinegar, honey or maple syrup, salt, and black pepper.
3. Lightly coat the air fryer basket with cooking spray or brush with olive oil.
4. Place the Brussels sprouts in the air fryer basket.
5. Air fry at 200°C for 12-15 minutes, shaking the basket halfway through, until the sprouts are tender and caramelized.
6. Once done, remove from the air fryer and serve.

## Crispy Air Fried Polenta Bites with Marinara Dip

Serves: 4
Prep time: 15 minutes / Cook time: 20 minutes

**Ingredients:**
- 300g polenta, cooked and cooled
- 50g grated Parmesan cheese
- 1 tsp Italian seasoning
- Cooking spray or olive oil spray
- Marinara sauce, for dipping

**Preparation instructions:**
1. Preheat the Air Fryer to 200°C for 5 minutes.
2. In a bowl, mix together cooked polenta, grated Parmesan cheese, and Italian seasoning.
3. Shape the polenta mixture into bite-sized squares or rounds.
4. Lightly coat the air fryer basket with cooking spray or brush with olive oil.
5. Place the polenta bites in the air fryer basket.
6. Air fry at 200°C for 15-20 minutes, turning halfway through, until golden and crispy.
7. Once done, remove from the air fryer and serve with marinara sauce for dipping.

## Paprika and Lime Air Fryer Corn on the Cob

Serves: 4
Prep time: 10 minutes / Cook time: 12 minutes

**Ingredients:**
- 4 corn on the cobs, husked and halved
- 2 tbsp melted butter
- Zest of 1 lime
- 1 tsp paprika
- Salt, to taste

**Preparation instructions:**
1. Preheat the Air Fryer to 200°C for 5 minutes.
2. In a bowl, mix melted butter, lime zest, paprika, and salt.
3. Brush the corn halves with the butter mixture.
4. Lightly coat the air fryer basket with cooking spray or brush with olive oil.
5. Place the corn on the cobs in the air fryer basket.
6. Air fry at 200°C for 10-12 minutes, turning halfway through, until the corn is cooked and lightly charred.
7. Once done, remove from the air fryer and serve.

## Air Fried Butternut Squash Fritters

Serves: 4
Prep time: 20 minutes / Cook time: 15 minutes

**Ingredients:**
- 500g butternut squash, peeled and grated
- 1 egg
- 50g breadcrumbs
- 2 tbsp chopped fresh parsley
- 1/2 tsp garlic powder
- Salt and black pepper, to taste
- Cooking spray or olive oil spray

**Preparation instructions:**
1. Preheat the Air Fryer to 200°C for 5 minutes.
2. In a bowl, mix together grated butternut squash, egg, breadcrumbs, chopped parsley, garlic powder, salt, and black pepper.
3. Shape the mixture into fritters.
4. Lightly coat the air fryer basket with cooking spray or brush with olive oil.
5. Place the butternut squash fritters in the air fryer basket.
6. Air fry at 200°C for 12-15 minutes, flipping halfway through, until golden and crispy.
7. Once done, remove from the air fryer and serve.

## TORTILLA CHIPS

Serves 2
Prep time: 10 minutes / Cook time: 10 minutes

- 4 corn tortillas
- Salt, to taste
- Cooking spray

**Preparation instructions:**
1. Preheat the air fryer to 350 degrees.
2. Stack the tortillas, and slice them horizontally and vertically into four triangles each. In batches arrange the tortilla pieces in the air fryer basket in a single layer.
3. Spritz each tortilla piece generously with the cooking spray, and sprinkle with salt. Cook in the air fryer for 10 minutes.
4. Remove the tortilla slices from the air fryer once they are crispy, and serve with salsa, if desired.

## RANCH MOZZARELLA STICKS

Serves 4
Prep time: 10 minutes / Cook time: 35 minutes

**Ingredients:**
- 250g all-purpose flour
- 1 tsp baking soda
- 2 eggs
- 1 tbsp whole milk
- 1 cup seasoned bread crumbs
- 8 mozzarella string cheese sticks
- 120ml marinara sauce

**Preparation instructions:**
1. Mix the flour and baking soda in a dish. Whisk the eggs and milk together in a separate dish, and pour the bread crumbs into a third dish.
2. Coat the cheese sticks in the flour and baking soda mixture, and then, the egg mixture. Dredge in the breadcrumbs, and freeze for 30 minutes.
3. Preheat the air fryer to 400 degrees.
4. Lightly spritz with cooking spray, and arrange 4 sticks in the air fryer basket to cook for 5 minutes.
5. Repeat the process with the rest of the cheese sticks, and serve with the marinara sauce.

## Bruschetta with Tomato and Basil

Serves: 4
Prep time: 15 minutes / Cook Time: 5 minutes

**Ingredients:**
- 4 slices of baguette or Italian bread
- 2 large tomatoes, diced
- 2 cloves of garlic, minced
- 8 fresh basil leaves, torn
- 2 tablespoons extra virgin olive oil
- Salt and pepper, to taste
- Balsamic glaze, for drizzling (optional)

**Preparation instructions:**
1. Preheat the air fryer medium-high heat.
2. Place the slices of bread on a baking sheet and toast them under the air fryer broiler for about 2-3 minutes on each side until lightly golden and crisp.
3. In a bowl, combine the diced tomatoes, minced garlic, torn basil leaves, and extra virgin olive oil. Season with salt and pepper to taste. Toss well to combine.
4. Remove the toasted bread from the air fryer oven and let it cool slightly.
5. Rub each slice of bread with a clove of garlic to impart a subtle garlic flavour.
6. Spoon the tomato and basil mixture onto each bread slice, spreading it evenly.
7. Drizzle with balsamic glaze, if desired, for added sweetness and tanginess.
8. Serve the bruschetta with tomato and basil immediately as an appetiser or light snack.

## Authentic Scotch Eggs

Serves 6
Prep time: 15 minutes / Cook time: 11 to 13 minutes

**Ingredients:**
- 680 g bulk lean chicken or turkey sausage
- 3 raw eggs, divided
- 355 ml dried breadcrumbs, divided
- 120 ml plain flour
- 6 hardboiled eggs, peeled
- Cooking oil spray

**Preparation instructions:**
1. In a large bowl, combine the chicken sausage, 1 raw egg, and 120 ml of breadcrumbs and mix well. Divide the mixture into 6 pieces and flatten each into a long oval.
2. In a shallow bowl, beat the remaining 2 raw eggs.
3. Place the flour in a small bowl.

4. Place the remaining 240 ml of breadcrumbs in a second small bowl.
5. Roll each hardboiled egg in the flour and wrap one of the chicken sausage pieces around each egg to encircle it completely.
6. One at a time, roll the encased eggs in the flour, dip in the beaten eggs, and finally dip in the breadcrumbs to coat.
7. Insert the crisper plate into the basket and the basket into the unit. Preheat the unit by selecting AIR FRY, setting the temperature to 192°C, and setting the time to 3 minutes. Select START/STOP to begin.
8. Once the unit is preheated, spray the crisper plate with cooking oil. Place the eggs in a single layer into the basket and spray them with oil.
9. Select AIR FRY, set the temperature to 192°C, and set the time to 13 minutes. Select START/STOP to begin.
10. After about 6 minutes, use tongs to turn the eggs and spray them with more oil. Resume cooking for 5 to 7 minutes more, or until the chicken is thoroughly cooked and the Scotch eggs are browned.
11. When the cooking is complete, serve warm.

## Rumaki

Makes about 24 rumaki
Prep time: 30 minutes / Cook time: 10 to 12 minutes per batch

**Ingredients:**
- 283 g raw chicken livers
- 1 can sliced water chestnuts, drained
- 60 ml low-salt teriyaki sauce
- 12 slices turkey bacon

**Preparation instructions:**
1. Cut livers into 1½-inch pieces, trimming out tough veins as you slice.
2. Place livers, water chestnuts, and teriyaki sauce in small container with lid. If needed, add another tablespoon of teriyaki sauce to make sure livers are covered. Refrigerate for 1 hour.
3. When ready to cook, cut bacon slices in half crosswise.
4. Wrap 1 piece of liver and 1 slice of water chestnut in each bacon strip. Secure with toothpick.
5. When you have wrapped half of the livers, place them in the air fryer basket in a single layer.
6. Air fry at 200°C for 10 to 12 minutes, until liver is done, and bacon is crispy.
7. While first batch cooks, wrap the remaining livers. Repeat step 6 to cook your second batch.

## Porridge Bread

Serves 6-8
Prep time: 10 minutes / Cook time: 35-40 minutes

**Ingredients:**
- 200 g rolled oats
- 200 g wholemeal flour
- 1 tsp baking soda
- 1 tsp salt
- 300 ml buttermilk

**Preparation instructions:**
1. Preheat your air fryer to 180°C.
2. In a large bowl, mix together the rolled oats, wholemeal flour, baking soda, and salt.
3. Pour in the buttermilk and stir well to combine.
4. Grease a 7-inch (18 cm) round cake pan and transfer the dough to the pan.
5. Smooth the top of the dough with a spatula and sprinkle with additional rolled oats if desired.
6. Place the pan in the air fryer basket and cook for 35-40 minutes or until the bread is golden brown and a toothpick inserted into the center comes out clean.
7. Remove the pan from the air fryer and let the bread cool for a few minutes before slicing and serving.

# Chapter 7: Vegan And Veggie

## Air Fried Vegan Falafel Patties

Serves: 4
Prep time: 15 minutes / Cook time: 15 minutes

**Ingredients:**
- 400g canned chickpeas, drained and rinsed
- 1 small onion, finely chopped
- 2 cloves garlic, minced
- 2 tbsp chopped fresh parsley
- 1 tsp ground cumin
- 1 tsp ground coriander
- 2 tbsp chickpea flour
- Salt and black pepper, to taste
- Cooking spray or olive oil spray

**Preparation instructions:**
1. Preheat the Air Fryer to 200°C for 5 minutes.
2. In a food processor, combine chickpeas, chopped onion, minced garlic, parsley, ground cumin, ground coriander, chickpea flour, salt, and black pepper. Pulse until the mixture is coarsely ground.
3. Shape the mixture into small patties.
4. Lightly coat the air fryer basket with cooking spray or brush with olive oil.
5. Place the falafel patties in the air fryer basket.
6. Air fry at 200°C for 12-15 minutes, flipping halfway through, until golden and crispy.
7. Once done, remove from the air fryer and serve.

## Crispy Stuffed Portobello Mushrooms with Spinach and Vegan Cheese

Serves: 4
Prep time: 20 minutes / Cook time: 12 minutes

**Ingredients:**
- 4 large Portobello mushrooms, stems removed
- 200g fresh spinach, chopped
- 150g vegan cheese, shredded
- 2 cloves garlic, minced
- 2 tbsp olive oil
- Salt and black pepper, to taste

**Preparation instructions:**
1. Preheat the Air Fryer to 180°C for 5 minutes.
2. In a pan, heat olive oil over medium heat. Add minced garlic and chopped spinach. Sauté until the spinach wilts. Season with salt and black pepper.
3. Stuff each Portobello mushroom with the sautéed spinach and top with vegan cheese.
4. Lightly coat the air fryer basket with cooking spray or brush with olive oil.
5. Place the stuffed Portobello mushrooms in the air fryer basket.
6. Air fry at 180°C for 10-12 minutes until the mushrooms are cooked through and the cheese is melted and bubbly.
7. Once done, remove from the air fryer and serve.

## Air Fryer Veggie Spring Rolls

Serves: 4
Prep time: 20 minutes / Cook time: 10 minutes

**Ingredients:**
- 8 spring roll wrappers
- 150g firm tofu, drained and thinly sliced
- 100g shredded cabbage
- 1 carrot, julienned
- 1/2 red bell pepper, thinly sliced
- 2 spring onions, thinly sliced
- 2 tbsp soy sauce
- 1 tbsp sesame oil
- 1 tsp cornstarch
- Cooking spray or olive oil spray

**Preparation instructions:**
1. In a bowl, mix together shredded cabbage, julienned carrot, sliced red bell pepper, and sliced spring onions. Add soy sauce, sesame oil, and cornstarch. Toss to combine.
2. Place a spring roll wrapper on a clean surface. Add a few slices of tofu and a spoonful of the vegetable mixture onto the wrapper.
3. Fold the sides of the wrapper over the filling, then roll it up tightly, sealing the edges with water.
4. Lightly coat the air fryer basket with cooking spray or brush with olive oil.
5. Place the veggie spring rolls in the air fryer

basket, seam side down.
6. Air fry at 180°C for 8-10 minutes, until crispy and golden.
7. Once done, remove from the air fryer and serve with your favorite dipping sauce.

## Vegan Buffalo Cauliflower Bites

Serves: 4
Prep time: 15 minutes / Cook time: 20 minutes

**Ingredients:**
- 1 head cauliflower, cut into florets
- 60g plain flour
- 120ml unsweetened almond milk
- 1 tsp garlic powder
- 1 tsp onion powder
- 1/2 tsp smoked paprika
- 120ml buffalo sauce
- Salt and black pepper, to taste
- Cooking spray or olive oil spray

**Preparation instructions:**
1. Preheat the Air Fryer to 200°C for 5 minutes.
2. In a bowl, mix together plain flour, almond milk, garlic powder, onion powder, smoked paprika, salt, and black pepper to form a batter.
3. Dip each cauliflower floret into the batter, ensuring it's coated well.
4. Lightly coat the air fryer basket with cooking spray or brush with olive oil.
5. Place the coated cauliflower florets in the air fryer basket in a single layer.
6. Air fry at 200°C for 15-20 minutes, flipping halfway through, until golden and crispy.
7. Once done, remove from the air fryer and toss the cauliflower bites in buffalo sauce.
8. Serve with your choice of dipping sauce.

## Air Fried Stuffed Peppers with Quinoa and Black Beans

Serves: 4
Prep time: 20 minutes / Cook time: 20 minutes

**Ingredients:**
- 4 large bell peppers, halved and seeds removed
- 200g cooked quinoa
- 200g canned black beans, drained and rinsed
- 1 onion, finely chopped
- 2 cloves garlic, minced
- 1 tsp ground cumin
- 1 tsp smoked paprika
- 100g chopped tomatoes
- Salt and black pepper, to taste
- Cooking spray or olive oil spray

**Preparation instructions:**
1. Preheat the Air Fryer to 180°C for 5 minutes.
2. In a pan, sauté onion and garlic until translucent. Add ground cumin, smoked paprika, chopped tomatoes, cooked quinoa, black beans, salt, and black pepper. Cook for a few minutes until well combined.
3. Lightly coat the air fryer basket with cooking spray or brush with olive oil.
4. Stuff each bell pepper half with the quinoa and black bean mixture.
5. Place the stuffed peppers in the air fryer basket.
6. Air fry at 180°C for 18-20 minutes, until the peppers are tender.
7. Once done, remove from the air fryer and serve.

## Chickpea and Spinach Vegan Tikka Masala

Serves: 4
Prep time: 20 minutes / Cook time: 20 minutes

**Ingredients:**
- 400g canned chickpeas, drained and rinsed
- 200g spinach leaves
- 1 onion, finely chopped
- 2 cloves garlic, minced
- 1-inch ginger, grated
- 400g chopped tomatoes
- 200ml coconut milk
- 2 tbsp tomato paste
- 1 tbsp garam masala
- 1 tsp ground turmeric
- 1 tsp ground cumin
- Salt and black pepper, to taste
- Fresh coriander leaves (optional, for garnish)
- Cooking spray or olive oil spray

**Preparation instructions:**
1. Preheat the Air Fryer to 180°C for 5 minutes.
2. In a pan, sauté onion, garlic, and ginger until softened. Add chopped tomatoes, tomato paste, garam masala, ground turmeric, ground cumin, salt, and black pepper. Cook for a few minutes.
3. Add chickpeas, spinach, and coconut milk to

the pan. Stir well to combine.
4. Lightly coat the air fryer basket with cooking spray or brush with olive oil.
5. Transfer the chickpea and spinach mixture to the air fryer basket.
6. Air fry at 180°C for 15-20 minutes, stirring occasionally, until the flavors combine and the sauce thickens.
7. Once done, remove from the air fryer, garnish with fresh coriander leaves if desired, and serve with rice or naan bread.

## Air Fryer Vegan Sweet Potato and Chickpea Curry

Serves: 4
Prep time: 15 minutes / Cook time: 20 minutes

**Ingredients:**
- 400g sweet potatoes, peeled and cubed
- 200g canned chickpeas, drained and rinsed
- 1 onion, chopped
- 2 cloves garlic, minced
- 1-inch ginger, grated
- 400ml coconut milk
- 200ml vegetable broth
- 2 tbsp curry powder
- 1 tbsp coconut oil
- Salt and black pepper, to taste
- Fresh coriander leaves (optional, for garnish)

**Preparation instructions:**
1. Preheat the Air Fryer to 180°C for 5 minutes.
2. In a pan, heat coconut oil over medium heat. Add chopped onions, garlic, and ginger. Sauté until onions are soft.
3. Add curry powder and stir for a minute.
4. Add sweet potatoes, chickpeas, coconut milk, and vegetable broth to the pan. Season with salt and black pepper.
5. Transfer the mixture to the air fryer basket.
6. Air fry at 180°C for 20 minutes, stirring occasionally, until sweet potatoes are tender and the curry thickens.
7. Once done, garnish with fresh coriander leaves if desired and serve with rice or naan bread.

## Crispy Coconut-Crusted Tofu Nuggets

Serves: 4
Prep time: 15 minutes / Cook time: 12 minutes

**Ingredients:**
- 300g firm tofu, pressed and cut into nugget-sized pieces
- 60g shredded coconut
- 40g breadcrumbs
- 2 tbsp cornstarch
- 1 tsp garlic powder
- 1 tsp onion powder
- Salt and black pepper, to taste
- Cooking spray or olive oil spray

**Preparation instructions:**
1. Preheat the Air Fryer to 200°C for 5 minutes.
2. In a bowl, mix shredded coconut, breadcrumbs, cornstarch, garlic powder, onion powder, salt, and black pepper.
3. Coat each tofu piece with the coconut mixture, pressing gently to adhere.
4. Lightly coat the air fryer basket with cooking spray or brush with olive oil.
5. Place the coated tofu nuggets in the air fryer basket in a single layer.
6. Air fry at 200°C for 10-12 minutes, flipping halfway through, until golden and crispy.
7. Once done, remove from the air fryer and serve with your favorite dipping sauce.

## Vegan Air Fried Courgette Fritters

Serves: 4
Prep time: 15 minutes / Cook time: 10 minutes

**Ingredients:**
- 2 medium courgettes (zucchinis), grated and excess liquid squeezed out
- 1 onion, grated
- 100g chickpea flour (gram flour)
- 2 tbsp nutritional yeast
- 1 tsp baking powder
- 1 tsp ground cumin
- Salt and black pepper, to taste
- Cooking spray or olive oil spray

**Preparation instructions:**
1. Preheat the Air Fryer to 200°C for 5 minutes.
2. In a bowl, combine grated courgettes, grated onion, chickpea flour, nutritional yeast, baking powder, ground cumin, salt, and black pepper to form a batter.
3. Lightly coat the air fryer basket with cooking spray or brush with olive oil.
4. Spoon portions of the batter into the air fryer basket to form fritters.
5. Air fry at 200°C for 8-10 minutes, flipping halfway through, until the fritters are golden brown and crispy.
6. Once done, remove from the air fryer and serve hot.

## Air Fryer Vegan Stuffed Grape Leaves

Serves: 4
Prep time: 30 minutes / Cook time: 15 minutes

**Ingredients:**
- 200g grape leaves (preserved in brine), drained
- 200g cooked rice
- 100g finely chopped tomatoes
- 50g finely chopped onions
- 50g chopped fresh parsley
- 50g chopped fresh mint
- 2 tbsp olive oil
- Juice of 1 lemon
- Salt and black pepper, to taste

**Preparation instructions:**
1. Preheat the Air Fryer to 180°C for 5 minutes.
2. In a bowl, mix together the cooked rice, chopped tomatoes, onions, parsley, mint, olive oil, lemon juice, salt, and black pepper to make the stuffing.
3. Place a grape leaf flat on a surface, vein-side up. Add a small spoonful of the stuffing in the center of the leaf.
4. Fold the sides of the leaf over the stuffing, then roll it up tightly.
5. Place the stuffed grape leaves in the air fryer basket.
6. Air fry at 180°C for 15 minutes or until the grape leaves are slightly crispy.
7. Once done, remove from the air fryer and let cool before serving.

## Vegan Air Fried Falafel Wraps with Tahini Sauce

Serves: 4
Prep time: 20 minutes / Cook time: 15 minutes

**Ingredients:**
- For Falafels:
- 400g canned chickpeas, drained and rinsed
- 1 small onion, chopped
- 3 cloves garlic, minced
- 2 tbsp chopped fresh parsley
- 1 tsp ground cumin
- 1 tsp ground coriander
- 2 tbsp chickpea flour (gram flour)
- Salt and black pepper, to taste
- Cooking spray or olive oil spray
- For Wraps:
- 4 whole wheat tortilla wraps
- Lettuce, tomato slices, cucumber slices (for filling)
- Tahini sauce (store-bought or homemade)

**Preparation instructions:**
1. Preheat the Air Fryer to 200°C for 5 minutes.
2. In a food processor, blend chickpeas, onion, garlic, parsley, cumin, coriander, chickpea flour, salt, and black pepper until a coarse paste forms.
3. Shape the mixture into small falafel balls.
4. Lightly coat the air fryer basket with cooking spray or brush with olive oil.
5. Place the falafel balls in the air fryer basket in a single layer.
6. Air fry at 200°C for 12-15 minutes, turning halfway through, until golden brown and crispy.
7. Warm the tortilla wraps, then fill them with lettuce, tomato, cucumber, air-fried falafels, and drizzle with tahini sauce. Roll them up and serve.

## Air Fried Vegan Onion Bhajis

Serves: 4
Prep time: 15 minutes / Cook time: 10 minutes

**Ingredients:**
- 200g gram flour (chickpea flour)
- 2 large onions, thinly sliced
- 1 tsp ground cumin
- 1 tsp ground coriander
- 1/2 tsp turmeric powder
- 1/2 tsp chili powder (adjust to taste)
- Salt, to taste

- Water (as needed)
- Cooking spray or olive oil spray

**Preparation instructions:**
1. Preheat the Air Fryer to 180°C for 5 minutes.
2. In a bowl, mix gram flour, sliced onions, ground cumin, ground coriander, turmeric powder, chili powder, and salt.
3. Gradually add water to the mixture to form a thick batter that coats the onions well.
4. Lightly coat the air fryer basket with cooking spray or brush with olive oil.
5. Spoon portions of the onion batter into the air fryer basket.
6. Air fry at 180°C for 8-10 minutes, turning halfway through, until golden and crispy.
7. Once done, remove from the air fryer and serve hot.

## Crispy Air Fryer Tofu Satay Skewers

Serves: 4
Prep time: 20 minutes / Cook time: 15 minutes

**Ingredients:**
- 400g firm tofu, pressed and cut into cubes
- 80ml soy sauce
- 3 tbsp peanut butter
- 2 tbsp lime juice
- 2 tbsp maple syrup
- 1 tsp minced garlic
- 1 tsp minced ginger
- 1/4 tsp chili flakes
- 8 wooden skewers, soaked in water

**Preparation instructions:**
1. Preheat the Air Fryer to 200°C for 5 minutes.
2. In a bowl, mix soy sauce, peanut butter, lime juice, maple syrup, minced garlic, minced ginger, and chili flakes to make the marinade.
3. Thread tofu cubes onto the soaked skewers.
4. Coat the tofu skewers with the marinade.
5. Place the skewers in the air fryer basket.
6. Air fry at 200°C for 12-15 minutes, turning halfway through, until the tofu is crispy and golden.
7. Once done, remove from the air fryer and let cool slightly before serving.

## Air Fried Vegan Breakfast Burritos

Serves: 4
Prep time: 15 minutes / Cook time: 15 minutes

**Ingredients:**
- 400g firm tofu, crumbled
- 1 onion, diced
- 2 garlic cloves, minced
- 1 red bell pepper, diced
- 1 tsp ground cumin
- 1 tsp ground turmeric
- Salt and black pepper, to taste
- 4 large tortilla wraps
- 200g cooked black beans
- 100g cooked brown rice
- Handful of fresh coriander, chopped
- Cooking spray or olive oil spray

**Preparation instructions:**
1. Preheat the Air Fryer to 180°C for 5 minutes.
2. In a skillet, sauté onion, garlic, and red bell pepper until softened.
3. Add crumbled tofu, ground cumin, ground turmeric, salt, and black pepper. Cook until tofu is heated through.
4. Lay out the tortilla wraps. Place a portion of the tofu scramble, black beans, brown rice, and fresh coriander on each wrap.
5. Roll up the wraps, folding in the sides to secure the filling, forming burritos.
6. Lightly coat the air fryer basket with cooking spray or olive oil.
7. Place the burritos in the air fryer basket, seam-side down.
8. Air fry at 180°C for 12-15 minutes until the burritos are crispy and golden.
9. Once done, remove from the air fryer and let cool for a minute before serving.

## Spicy Cauliflower Wings

Serves: 4
Prep time: 15 minutes / Cook time: 20 minutes

**Ingredients:**
- 1 head cauliflower, cut into florets
- 100g plain flour
- 120ml unsweetened plant-based milk

- 1 tsp garlic powder
- 1 tsp onion powder
- 1 tsp paprika
- 1/2 tsp cayenne pepper
- Salt and black pepper, to taste
- Cooking spray or olive oil spray
- 120ml hot sauce
- 2 tbsp melted vegan butter

**Preparation instructions:**
1. Preheat the Air Fryer to 200°C for 5 minutes.
2. In a bowl, mix flour, plant-based milk, garlic powder, onion powder, paprika, cayenne pepper, salt, and black pepper to create a batter.
3. Dip cauliflower florets into the batter, ensuring they're well coated.
4. Lightly coat the air fryer basket with cooking spray or olive oil.
5. Place the battered cauliflower in the air fryer basket in a single layer.
6. Air fry at 200°C for 15-18 minutes, flipping halfway through, until crispy and golden.
7. In another bowl, mix hot sauce and melted vegan butter.
8. Toss the cooked cauliflower in the hot sauce mixture until evenly coated.
9. Return the coated cauliflower to the air fryer for an additional 5 minutes.
10. Once done, remove from the air fryer and let cool for a few minutes before serving.

## Air-Fried Mediterranean Vegetables

Serves: 4
Prep time: 15 minutes / Cook time: 10 minutes

**Ingredients:**
- 1 red pepper, sliced
- 1 yellow pepper, sliced
- 1 small aubergine, diced
- 1 courgette, sliced
- 1 red onion, sliced
- 2 cloves of garlic, minced
- 2 tbsp olive oil
- 1 tsp dried oregano
- 1 tsp dried basil
- 1/2 tsp dried thyme
- Salt and black pepper, to taste
- Fresh parsley, chopped (for garnish)

**Preparation instructions:**
1. Preheat the air fryer to 200°C for 5 minutes.
2. In a large mixing bowl, combine the sliced red and yellow peppers, diced aubergine, sliced courgette, red onion, and minced garlic.
3. Drizzle the vegetables with olive oil and sprinkle with dried oregano, dried basil, dried thyme, salt, and black pepper. Toss until well-coated.
4. Place the seasoned vegetables in the air fryer basket in a single layer. If necessary, cook them in batches to avoid overcrowding.
5. Air fry the vegetables at 200°C for 12-15 minutes, shaking the basket halfway through the cooking time to ensure even cooking.
6. Once the vegetables are tender and slightly caramelised, remove them from the air fryer and transfer them to a serving dish.
7. Garnish with fresh parsley and serve hot as a delicious and healthy side dish.

## Brussels Sprouts with Balsamic Glaze

Serves: 4
Prep time: 10 minutes / Cook time: 15 minutes

**Ingredients:**
- 500g Brussels sprouts, trimmed and halved
- 2 tbsp olive oil
- 2 tbsp balsamic vinegar
- 1 tbsp honey
- Salt and black pepper, to taste
- Grated Parmesan cheese, for garnish (optional)

**Preparation instructions:**
1. Preheat the air fryer to 200°C for 5 minutes.
2. In a large mixing bowl, combine the Brussels sprouts, olive oil, balsamic vinegar, honey, salt, and black pepper. Toss until the Brussels sprouts are evenly coated.
3. Place the seasoned Brussels sprouts in the air fryer basket in a single layer. If necessary, cook them in batches to avoid overcrowding.
4. Air fry the Brussels sprouts at 200°C for 12-15 minutes, shaking the basket or tossing the sprouts halfway through the cooking time for even browning.
5. Once the Brussels sprouts are tender and caramelised, remove them from the air fryer

and transfer them to a serving dish.
6. Optional: Sprinkle the air-fried Brussels sprouts with grated Parmesan cheese for added flavour and richness.
7. Serve the air-fried Brussels sprouts with balsamic glaze hot as a delectable and healthy side dish.

## Curried Fruit

Serves 6 to 8
Prep time: 10 minutes / Cook time: 20 minutes

**Ingredients:**
- 210 g cubed fresh pineapple
- 200 g cubed fresh pear (firm, not overly ripe)
- 230 g frozen peaches, thawed
- 425 g can dark, sweet, pitted cherries with juice
- 2 tablespoons brown sugar
- 1 teaspoon curry powder

**Preparation instructions:**
1. Combine all Ingredients: in large bowl. Stir gently to mix in the sugar and curry.
2. Pour into a baking pan and bake at 180°C for 10 minutes.
3. Stir fruit and cook 10 more minutes. 4. Serve hot.

## Roasted Aubergine

Serves 4
Prep time: 15 minutes / Cook time: 15 minutes

**Ingredients:**
- 1 large aubergine
- 2 tablespoons olive oil
- ¼ teaspoon salt
- ½ teaspoon garlic powder

**Preparation instructions:**
1. Remove top and bottom from aubergine. Slice aubergine into ¼-inch-thick round slices. 2. Brush slices with olive oil. Sprinkle with salt and garlic powder. Place aubergine slices into the air fryer basket.
3. Adjust the temperature to 200°C and set the timer for 15 minutes.
4. Serve immediately.

## Air Fryer Sweet Potato and Black Bean Cakes

Serves 4
Prep Time 20 minutes / Cook Time 15 minutes

**Ingredients:**
- 2 sweet potatoes, cooked and mashed
- 400g canned black beans, drained and rinsed
- 1 onion, finely chopped
- 2 cloves garlic, minced
- 1 teaspoon ground cumin
- Salt and pepper to taste
2 tablespoons flour

**Preparation instructions:**
1. In a large bowl, mix together the sweet potatoes, black beans, onion, garlic, cumin, salt, and pepper.
2. Stir in the flour. Shape the mixture into small cakes.
3. Place the cakes in the air fryer basket.
4. Cook at 180°C for 15 minutes, turning halfway through, until the cakes are golden brown and crispy.

# Chapter 8: Sweet Snacks And Desserts

## Air Fryer Apple Cinnamon Fritters

Serves: 4
Prep time: 15 minutes / Cook time: 15 minutes

**Ingredients:**
- 200g plain flour
- 30g granulated sugar
- 1 tsp baking powder
- 1/2 tsp ground cinnamon
- 1/4 tsp salt
- 1 large egg
- 120ml milk
- 2 apples, peeled, cored, and diced
- Oil spray

**Preparation instructions:**
1. Preheat the Air Fryer to 180°C for 5 minutes.
2. In a bowl, mix flour, sugar, baking powder, cinnamon, and salt.
3. In another bowl, beat the egg and milk together, then add to the dry Ingredients:, stirring until smooth.
4. Gently fold in the diced apples into the batter.
5. Lightly coat the air fryer basket with oil spray.
6. Drop spoonfuls of the batter into the basket, leaving space between each fritter.
7. Air fry at 180°C for 10-12 minutes until golden brown and cooked through, flipping halfway through.
8. Once done, remove from the air fryer and let cool for a minute before serving.

## Chocolate-stuffed Air Fried Croissants

Serves: 4
Prep time: 10 minutes / Cook time: 10 minutes

**Ingredients:**
- 4 mini croissants
- 60g chocolate chips or chocolate chunks
- Icing sugar (for dusting)

**Preparation instructions:**
1. Preheat the Air Fryer to 180°C for 5 minutes.
2. Slice each mini croissant open without cutting completely in half.
3. Stuff each croissant with chocolate chips or chunks.
4. Place the croissants in the air fryer basket.
5. Air fry at 180°C for 5-6 minutes until the croissants are crispy and the chocolate is melted.
6. Remove from the air fryer and let cool slightly.
7. Dust with icing sugar before serving.

## Air Fried Banoffee Pie Bites

Serves: 4
Prep time: 15 minutes / Cook time: 12 minutes

**Ingredients:**
- 4 small ripe bananas, sliced
- 100g digestive biscuits, crushed
- 60g butter, melted
- 120g dulce de leche or caramel sauce
- Whipped cream (optional)
- Chocolate shavings (optional)

**Preparation instructions:**
1. Preheat the Air Fryer to 180°C for 5 minutes.
2. Mix the crushed digestive biscuits with melted butter until well combined.
3. Press the biscuit mixture into the bottom of silicone muffin cups or a mold to form a base.
4. Layer slices of banana over the biscuit base.
5. Top each with a dollop of dulce de leche or caramel sauce.
6. Air fry at 180°C for 10-12 minutes until the edges are golden brown.
7. Remove from the air fryer and let cool slightly.
8. Top with whipped cream and chocolate shavings if desired before serving.

## Sticky Toffee Pudding Cups

Serves: 4
Prep time: 15 minutes / Cook time: 15 minutes

**Ingredients:**
- 200g pitted dates, chopped
- 200ml boiling water

- 1 tsp vanilla extract
- 60g unsalted butter, softened
- 100g light brown sugar
- 2 large eggs
- 200g self-raising flour
- 1 tsp baking powder
- 60ml milk
- For the Toffee Sauce:
- 100g light brown sugar
- 100g unsalted butter
- 150ml double cream

**Preparation instructions:**
1. Preheat the Air Fryer to 180°C for 5 minutes.
2. In a bowl, pour boiling water over the chopped dates and let sit for 10 minutes. Then, mash the dates with a fork and stir in vanilla extract.
3. In another bowl, cream together softened butter and brown sugar. Add eggs one at a time, mixing well after each addition.
4. Sift in the self-raising flour and baking powder into the butter mixture. Stir in the date mixture and milk until combined.
5. Divide the batter equally among 4 silicone cups or molds.
6. Air fry at 180°C for 12-15 minutes until a toothpick inserted comes out clean.

**For the Toffee Sauce:**
1. In a saucepan, melt butter and sugar over low heat.
2. Stir in the double cream and let it simmer for a few minutes until slightly thickened.
3. Drizzle the warm toffee sauce over the individual pudding cups before serving.

## Air Fryer Lemon Blueberry Scones

Serves: 4
Prep time: 15 minutes / Cook time: 12 minutes

**Ingredients:**
- 250g self-raising flour
- 50g caster sugar
- 60g unsalted butter, chilled and cubed
- 125ml milk
- Zest of 1 lemon
- 100g fresh blueberries

**Preparation instructions:**
1. Preheat the Air Fryer to 180°C for 5 minutes.
2. In a bowl, mix the self-raising flour and sugar. Rub in the chilled butter until the mixture resembles breadcrumbs.
3. Stir in the milk, lemon zest, and fresh blueberries until the dough forms.
4. Gently pat the dough into a round on a floured surface and cut into 4 wedges.
5. Place the scones on the air fryer tray.
6. Air fry at 180°C for 10-12 minutes until the scones are golden brown.

## Vegan Air Fried Donuts with Raspberry Glaze

Serves: 4
Prep time: 15 minutes / Cook time: 10 minutes

**Ingredients:**
- 250g plain flour
- 50g caster sugar
- 1 tsp baking powder
- 1/4 tsp baking soda
- 1/2 tsp ground cinnamon
- 120ml unsweetened almond milk
- 60ml vegetable oil
- 1 tsp vanilla extract
- For the Raspberry Glaze:
- 100g icing sugar
- 2-3 tbsp raspberry puree (strained)

**Preparation instructions:**
1. Preheat the Air Fryer to 180°C for 5 minutes.
2. In a bowl, whisk together flour, sugar, baking powder, baking soda, and cinnamon.
3. Add almond milk, vegetable oil, and vanilla extract to the dry Ingredients:, mixing until a soft dough forms.
4. Roll the dough out on a floured surface to about 1/2 inch thickness and cut out donut shapes using a cutter.
5. Place the donuts in the air fryer basket, ensuring they have space between them.
6. Air fry at 180°C for 5-7 minutes until golden brown.

**For the Raspberry Glaze:**
1. Mix the icing sugar with enough raspberry puree to create a thick glaze.
2. Dip the cooled donuts into the raspberry glaze and let them set for a few minutes before serving.

## Air Fryer Baklava Rolls

Serves: 4
Prep time: 15 minutes / Cook time: 12 minutes

**Ingredients:**
- 150g chopped mixed nuts (walnuts, almonds, pistachios)
- 50g caster sugar
- 1 tsp ground cinnamon
- 100g melted unsalted butter
- 8 sheets of filo pastry
- 100g honey

**Preparation instructions:**
1. Preheat the Air Fryer to 180°C for 5 minutes.
2. In a bowl, mix the chopped nuts, sugar, and cinnamon together.
3. Lay out a sheet of filo pastry and brush it lightly with melted butter. Repeat with 3 more sheets, layering and brushing butter in between.
4. Sprinkle the nut mixture over the top layer of filo.
5. Roll the pastry into a log and cut into smaller rolls.
6. Place the rolls into the air fryer basket and air fry at 180°C for 10-12 minutes until golden.
7. Warm the honey and drizzle it over the baklava rolls before serving.

## Mini Victoria Sponge Cakes

Serves: 4
Prep time: 20 minutes / Cook time: 15 minutes

**Ingredients:**
- 150g unsalted butter, softened
- 150g caster sugar
- 3 large eggs
- 150g self-raising flour
- 1 tsp baking powder
- Raspberry jam
- 100ml double cream, whipped
- Icing sugar for dusting

**Preparation instructions:**
1. Preheat the Air Fryer to 180°C for 5 minutes.
2. In a bowl, cream the butter and sugar until pale and fluffy. Add eggs one at a time, beating well after each addition.
3. Sift in the self-raising flour and baking powder, folding until combined.
4. Divide the batter into silicone muffin cups or molds.
5. Air fry at 180°C for 12-15 minutes until risen and golden.
6. Once cooled, slice the cakes in half, spread raspberry jam, add a dollop of whipped cream, and sandwich them together.
7. Dust the tops with icing sugar before serving.

## Air Fryer Pear and Almond Tarts

Serves: 4
Prep time: 20 minutes / Cook time: 15 minutes

**Ingredients:**
- 1 sheet ready-rolled puff pastry
- 2 ripe pears, thinly sliced
- 50g ground almonds
- 25g caster sugar
- 1 egg, beaten
- Flaked almonds for topping
- Honey for drizzling

**Preparation instructions:**
1. Preheat the Air Fryer to 180°C for 5 minutes.
2. Cut the puff pastry into 4 squares.
3. Score a border around each square, leaving a small border.
4. Mix the ground almonds and sugar together and sprinkle it inside the border of each square.
5. Arrange the pear slices over the almond mixture.
6. Brush the edges of the pastry with beaten egg and sprinkle flaked almonds over the pears.
7. Air fry at 180°C for 12-15 minutes until the pastry is golden and puffed.
8. Drizzle honey over the tarts before serving.

## Caramelized Banana Spring Rolls

Serves: 4
Prep time: 15 minutes / Cook time: 10 minutes

**Ingredients:**
- 4 spring roll wrappers
- 2 ripe bananas, sliced
- 50g brown sugar
- 30g unsalted butter, melted
- Icing sugar for dusting
- Vanilla ice cream (optional, for serving)

**Preparation instructions:**
1. Preheat the Air Fryer to 180°C for 5 minutes.
2. Place banana slices in the center of each spring roll wrapper, sprinkle with brown sugar, and roll them up.
3. Brush the spring rolls with melted butter.
4. Arrange the rolls in the air fryer basket.
5. Air fry at 180°C for 8-10 minutes or until golden and crispy.
6. Dust with icing sugar and serve with a scoop of vanilla ice cream if desired.

## Air Fried Sticky Rice Mango Pudding

Serves: 4
Prep time: 15 minutes / Cook time: 15 minutes

**Ingredients:**
- 200g glutinous rice, soaked for 4 hours
- 200ml coconut milk
- 50g sugar
- 1 ripe mango, diced
- Sesame seeds for garnish (optional)

**Preparation instructions:**
1. Drain the soaked glutinous rice and place it in the air fryer basket.
2. Air fry at 180°C for 8 minutes, shaking the basket halfway through to ensure even cooking.
3. In a bowl, mix together the coconut milk and sugar until the sugar dissolves.
4. Pour the coconut milk mixture over the cooked rice in the air fryer.
5. Add diced mango on top.
6. Air fry at 180°C for an additional 7 minutes until the mango is slightly caramelized.
7. Serve warm, garnished with sesame seeds if desired.

## Blueberry-Lemon Bread Pudding

Serves: 4
Prep time: 15 minutes / Cook time: 20 minutes

**Ingredients:**
- 4 slices of bread, cubed
- 200g fresh blueberries
- Zest of 1 lemon
- 300ml whole milk
- 2 large eggs
- 50g sugar
- 1 tsp vanilla extract
- Icing sugar for dusting

**Preparation instructions:**
1. Preheat the Air Fryer to 180°C for 5 minutes.
2. In a bowl, combine the bread cubes, blueberries, and lemon zest.
3. In another bowl, whisk together the milk, eggs, sugar, and vanilla extract.
4. Pour the egg mixture over the bread and blueberries, ensuring everything is coated.
5. Transfer the mixture to a greased air fryer-safe dish that fits into the basket.
6. Air fry at 180°C for 18-20 minutes or until the top is golden brown and the pudding is set.
7. Dust with icing sugar before serving.

## Air Fryer Raspberry White Chocolate Cookies

Serves: 4
Prep time: 15 minutes / Cook time: 10 minutes

**Ingredients:**
- 100g unsalted butter, softened
- 100g caster sugar
- 1 large egg
- 1 tsp vanilla extract
- 200g plain flour
- 1/2 tsp baking powder
- 50g white chocolate chips
- 50g fresh raspberries, chopped

**Preparation instructions:**
1. In a bowl, cream together the softened butter and caster sugar until light and fluffy.
2. Beat in the egg and vanilla extract until well combined.
3. Sift the flour and baking powder into the mixture, then fold in the white chocolate chips and chopped raspberries.
4. Shape the cookie dough into small balls and place them in the air fryer basket lined with parchment paper.
5. Flatten the dough balls slightly with your fingers.
6. Air fry at 160°C for 8-10 minutes or until the edges are golden brown.
7. Allow the cookies to cool before serving.

## Air Fried Chocolate Covered Strawberries

Serves: 4
Prep time: 10 minutes / Cook time: 5 minutes

**Ingredients:**
- 200g fresh strawberries, washed and dried
- 100g milk chocolate, chopped
- 50g white chocolate, chopped (optional, for decoration)

**Preparation instructions:**
1. Place the chopped milk chocolate in a microwave-safe bowl and melt it in 30-second intervals, stirring in between until smooth.
2. Dip each strawberry into the melted chocolate, coating them halfway.
3. Place the chocolate-coated strawberries in the air fryer basket lined with parchment paper.
4. Air fry at 160°C for 4-5 minutes until the chocolate is set.
5. If using, melt the white chocolate and drizzle it over the cooled chocolate-covered strawberries.
6. Let them set before serving.

## Apple Crumble Stuffed Baked Apples

Serves: 4
Prep time: 15 minutes / Cook time: 20 minutes

**Ingredients:**
- 4 large apples, cored
- 50g rolled oats
- 50g plain flour
- 50g unsalted butter, diced
- 40g brown sugar
- 1/2 tsp ground cinnamon
- Vanilla ice cream or custard, for serving (optional)

**Preparation instructions:**
1. In a bowl, mix together the rolled oats, flour, diced butter, brown sugar, and ground cinnamon until it resembles coarse crumbs.
2. Fill the cored apples with the crumble mixture, packing it gently.
3. Place the stuffed apples in the air fryer basket.
4. Air fry at 180°C for 18-20 minutes until the apples are tender and the crumble is golden.
5. Serve warm with a scoop of vanilla ice cream or custard if desired.

## Air Fried Churro Bites with Cinnamon Sugar

Serves: 4
Prep time: 15 minutes / Cook time: 8 minutes

**Ingredients:**
- 100g plain flour
- 100ml water
- 50g unsalted butter
- 2 tbsp caster sugar
- 1/2 tsp ground cinnamon
- Pinch of salt
- Vegetable oil spray

**Preparation instructions:**
1. In a saucepan, combine water, butter, sugar, cinnamon, and salt. Bring it to a boil, then reduce the heat.
2. Add the flour and mix vigorously until the dough forms and pulls away from the sides of the pan. Remove from heat.
3. Let the dough cool slightly, then transfer it to a piping bag fitted with a star tip.
4. Pipe 2-3cm strips of dough into the air fryer basket lined with parchment paper, cutting them with scissors, and leaving space between each one.
5. Lightly spray the churro bites with vegetable oil.
6. Air fry at 180°C for 6-8 minutes or until golden brown and crisp.
7. In a bowl, mix caster sugar and cinnamon. Coat the warm churro bites in the sugar mixture before serving.

## Air Fryer Pecan Pie Pockets

Serves: 4
Prep time: 20 minutes / Cook time: 12 minutes

**Ingredients:**
- 1 sheet ready-rolled shortcrust pastry, thawed
- 100g pecans, chopped
- 50g brown sugar
- 50g golden syrup
- 50g unsalted butter, melted
- 1 tsp vanilla extract
- 1/2 tsp ground cinnamon
- 1/4 tsp salt
- 1 large egg, beaten (for egg wash)

**Preparation instructions:**
1. Preheat the Air Fryer to 180°C for 5 minutes.

2. In a bowl, mix together the chopped pecans, brown sugar, golden syrup, melted butter, vanilla extract, cinnamon, and salt.
3. Roll out the shortcrust pastry and cut it into squares.
4. Spoon a portion of the pecan mixture into the center of each pastry square.
5. Brush the edges of the pastry squares with beaten egg and fold them over to form pockets, pressing the edges firmly to seal.
6. Place the pockets in the air fryer basket lined with parchment paper.
7. Air fry at 180°C for 10-12 minutes or until golden brown and cooked through.

## Vegan Air Fried Coconut Macaroons

Serves: 4
Prep time: 10 minutes / Cook time: 12 minutes

**Ingredients:**
- 150g shredded coconut
- 100g aquafaba (liquid from canned chickpeas)
- 50g caster sugar
- 1/2 tsp vanilla extract
- 50g dairy-free chocolate, melted (optional, for drizzling)

**Preparation instructions:**
1. In a bowl, whisk aquafaba until it forms soft peaks.
2. Gently fold in shredded coconut, caster sugar, and vanilla extract until well combined.
3. Scoop spoonfuls of the mixture onto the air fryer tray lined with parchment paper, shaping them into small mounds.
4. Air fry at 160°C for 10-12 minutes or until the macaroons are golden and firm.
5. Optional: Drizzle melted dairy-free chocolate over the cooled macaroons.
6. Let them cool completely before serving.

## Air Fryer Orange Glazed Madeleines

Serves: 4
Prep time: 15 minutes / Cook time: 8 minutes

**Ingredients:**
- 100g plain flour
- 2 large eggs
- 80g caster sugar
- 1/2 tsp baking powder
- Zest of 1 orange
- 60g unsalted butter, melted
- 1 tsp vanilla extract
- For the Glaze:
- 100g icing sugar
- 2-3 tbsp freshly squeezed orange juice

**Preparation instructions:**
1. Preheat the Air Fryer to 180°C for 5 minutes.
2. In a bowl, whisk eggs and caster sugar until pale and fluffy.
3. Add the orange zest, melted butter, and vanilla extract, mixing until well combined.
4. Sift in the flour and baking powder, folding gently until the batter is smooth.
5. Grease the madeleine molds if they are not silicone, then spoon the batter into each mold, filling about 3/4 full.
6. Place the madeleine molds in the Air Fryer basket.
7. Air fry at 180°C for 6-8 minutes until the madeleines are golden brown and spring back when touched.
8. For the glaze, mix icing sugar with freshly squeezed orange juice until it forms a smooth, thick glaze.
9. Dip the cooled madeleines into the glaze and let them set on a wire rack.

## Peach and Raspberry Galette

Serves: 4
Prep time: 20 minutes / Cook time: 25 minutes

**Ingredients:**
- 1 ready-made puff pastry sheet (about 320g)
- 2 peaches, sliced
- 100g fresh raspberries
- 30g granulated sugar
- 1 tbsp cornflour
- 1 tbsp milk
- 1 tbsp demerara sugar (for sprinkling)
- Optional: Vanilla ice cream or whipped cream for serving

**Preparation instructions:**
1. Preheat the Air Fryer to 180°C for 5 minutes.
2. In a bowl, gently toss sliced peaches, raspberries, granulated sugar, and cornflour

together until the fruit is coated.
3. Roll out the puff pastry on a lightly floured surface into a circle or rectangle, about 0.5cm thick.
4. Transfer the pastry to the Air Fryer basket lined with parchment paper.
5. Arrange the fruit mixture in the center of the pastry, leaving a border around the edges.
6. Gently fold the edges of the pastry over the fruit, creating pleats as you go around.
7. Brush the pastry edges with milk and sprinkle demerara sugar on top.
8. Air fry at 180°C for 20-25 minutes until the pastry is golden and the fruits are tender.
9. Serve warm with a scoop of vanilla ice cream or whipped cream if desired.

## Baked Apples and Walnuts

Serves 4

Prep time: 6 minutes / Cook time: 20 minutes

**Ingredients:**
- 4 small Granny Smith apples
- 50 g chopped walnuts
- 50 g light brown sugar
- 2 tablespoons butter, melted
- 1 teaspoon ground cinnamon
- ½ teaspoon ground nutmeg
- 120 ml water, or apple juice

**Preparation instructions:**
1. Cut off the top third of the apples. Spoon out the core and some of the flesh and discard. Place the apples in a small air fryer baking pan.
2. Insert the crisper plate into the basket and the basket into the unit. Preheat to 176°C.
3. In a small bowl, stir together the walnuts, brown sugar, melted butter, cinnamon, and nutmeg. Spoon this mixture into the centers of the hollowed-out apples.
4. Once the unit is preheated, pour the water into the crisper plate. Place the baking pan into the basket.
5. Bake for 20 minutes. 6. When the cooking is complete, the apples should be bubbly and fork tender.

## Brown Sugar Banana Bread

Serves 4

Prep time: 20 minutes / Cook time: 22 to 24 minutes

**Ingredients:**
- 195 g packed light brown sugar
- 1 large egg, beaten
- 2 tablespoons unsalted butter, melted
- 120 ml milk, whole or semi-skimmed
- 250 g plain flour
- 1½ teaspoons baking powder
- 1 teaspoon ground cinnamon
- ½ teaspoon salt
- 1 banana, mashed
- 1 to 2 tablespoons coconut, or avocado oil oil
- 30 g icing sugar (optional)

**Preparation instructions:**
1. In a large bowl, stir together the brown sugar, egg, melted butter, and milk.
2. In a medium bowl, whisk the flour, baking powder, cinnamon, and salt until blended. Add the flour mixture to the sugar mixture and stir just to blend.
3. Add the mashed banana and stir to combine.
4. Preheat the air fryer to 176°C. Spritz 2 mini loaf pans with oil.
5. Evenly divide the batter between the prepared pans and place them in the air fryer basket.
6. Cook for 22 to 24 minutes, or until a knife inserted into the middle of the loaves comes out clean.
7. Dust the warm loaves with icing sugar (if using).

# References

Air Fryer Recipes. (n.d.-a). Allrecipes. https://www.allrecipes.com/recipes/23070/everyday-cooking/cookware-and-equipment/air-fryer/

Air fryer recipes. (n.d.-b). BBC Food. Retrieved December 22, 2023, from https://www.bbc.co.uk/food/collections/air_fryer_recipes

Air-Fryer Recipes. (n.d.). Tesco Real Food. Retrieved December 22, 2023, from https://realfood.tesco.com/category/air-fryer.html

Doster, N. (n.d.). 82 Air-Fryer Recipes You Need to Try. Taste of Home. https://www.tasteofhome.com/collection/air-fryer-recipes/

Green, L. (2023, August 24). 47 Air Fryer Recipes (With Easy To Follow Steps!). Liana's Kitchen. https://lianaskitchen.co.uk/air-fryer-recipes/

JamieOliver.com. (n.d.). Air-fryer recipes / Jamie Oliver. Jamie Oliver. Retrieved December 22, 2023, from https://www.jamieoliver.com/recipes/air-fryer-recipes/

Samantha. (2021, August 19). 65 Easy Air Fryer Recipes for Beginners. Everyday Family Cooking. https://www.everydayfamilycooking.com/air-fryer-recipes-for-beginners/

Printed in Great Britain
by Amazon